INTERNATIONAL E

Energy Policies
of IEA Countries

THE UNITED
KINGDOM

2006 Review

INTERNATIONAL ENERGY AGENCY

The International Energy Agency (IEA) is an autonomous body which was established in November 1974 within the framework of the Organisation for Economic Co-operation and Development (OECD) to implement an international energy programme.

It carries out a comprehensive programme of energy co-operation among twenty-six of the OECD's thirty member countries. The basic aims of the IEA are:

- To maintain and improve systems for coping with oil supply disruptions.
- To promote rational energy policies in a global context through co-operative relations with non-member countries, industry and international organisations.
- To operate a permanent information system on the international oil market.
- To improve the world's energy supply and demand structure by developing alternative energy sources and increasing the efficiency of energy use.
- To assist in the integration of environmental and energy policies.

The IEA member countries are: Australia, Austria, Belgium, Canada, the Czech Republic, Denmark, Finland, France, Germany, Greece, Hungary, Ireland, Italy, Japan, the Republic of Korea, Luxembourg, the Netherlands, New Zealand, Norway, Portugal, Spain, Sweden, Switzerland, Turkey, the United Kingdom and the United States. The European Commission takes part in the work of the IEA.

ORGANISATION FOR ECONOMIC CO-OPERATION AND DEVELOPMENT

The OECD is a unique forum where the governments of thirty democracies work together to address the economic, social and environmental challenges of globalisation. The OECD is also at the forefront of efforts to understand and to help governments respond to new developments and concerns, such as corporate governance, the information economy and the challenges of an ageing population. The Organisation provides a setting where governments can compare policy experiences, seek answers to common problems, identify good practice and work to co-ordinate domestic and international policies.

The OECD member countries are: Australia, Austria, Belgium, Canada, the Czech Republic, Denmark, Finland, France, Germany, Greece, Hungary, Iceland, Ireland, Italy, Japan, Korea, Luxembourg, Mexico, the Netherlands, New Zealand, Norway, Poland, Portugal, the Slovak Republic, Spain, Sweden, Switzerland, Turkey, the United Kingdom and the United States. The European Commission takes part in the work of the OECD.

TABLE OF CONTENTS

Tables and Figures

TABLES

FIGURES

ORGANISATION OF THE REVIEW

REVIEW TEAM

The 2006 IEA in-depth review of the energy policies of the United Kingdom (UK) was undertaken on 2-7 April 2006 by a team of energy specialists drawn from IEA member countries and the IEA Secretariat. Meetings were held with government officials, energy suppliers, energy consumers and public interest groups. This report was drafted on the basis of those meetings and the government's official response to the IEA's policy questionnaire. The team greatly appreciates the openness and co-operation shown by everyone it met.

The members of the team were:

David Pumphrey (team leader)
Department of Energy
The United States

Ian Hayhow
Natural Resources Canada
Canada

Ritva Hirvonen
Energy Market Authority
Finland

Morten Møller
Danish Energy Authority
Denmark

Giordano Rigon
Directorate-General for Energy
and Transport
European Commission

Evelyne Bertel
Nuclear Energy Agency

Jeppe Bjerg
Energy Technology Office
IEA

Ulrik Stridbaek
Energy Diversification Division
IEA

Jun Arima
Head, Country Studies Division
IEA

Jonathan Coony
Country Studies Division
IEA

Jonathan Coony managed the review and wrote the report with the exception of the electricity chapter which was written by Ulrik Stridbaek, the nuclear energy chapter which was written by Evelyne Bertel and the R&D chapter which was written by Jeppe Bjerg. Monica Petit and Bertrand Sadin prepared the figures, and Marilyn Ferris provided editorial assistance.

ORGANISATIONS VISITED

The team held discussions with the following groups:

- Department of Trade and Industry (DTI)
- Department for Environment, Food and Rural Affairs
- Office of Gas and Electricity Markets (Ofgem)
- National Grid
- The Carbon Trust
- British Energy
- Centrica
- Energy Savings Trust
- The British Energy Efficiency Federation (BEEF)
- Energy Efficiency Partnership for Homes
- The Local Government Association (LGA)
- Lewisham Council
- Association of Energy Producers
- British Petroleum
- International Power
- EDF Energy
- RWE npower
- Shell International, Ltd
- Ernst & Young
- Futures and Options Association (FOA)
- The Engineering and Physical Sciences Research Council (EPSRC)
- The UK Energy Research Centre (UKERC)
- Energywatch
- The Stern Review on the Economics of Climate Change
- The Business Council for Sustainable Energy UK
- Combined Heat & Power Association

REVIEW CRITERIA

The IEA *Shared Goals*, which were adopted by the IEA Ministers at their 4 June 1993 meeting in Paris, provide the evaluation criteria for the in-depth reviews conducted by the IEA. The *Shared Goals* are set out in Annex B.

SUMMARY OF CONCLUSIONS AND RECOMMENDATIONS

The IEA in-depth review of the energy policy of the United Kingdom focuses on two major themes. The first is the market's ability to provide for security of energy supply or, alternatively, the need for government to play a more active role in guaranteeing reliable supply. The second is energy efficiency and the government's policies to curb energy demand. While the review covers the entire spectrum of energy issues, the greatest attention is given to these two themes.

The UK government has been a pioneer in many aspects of energy policy. It was the first country to liberalise gas and electricity markets through privatisation, competition and open access to networks. The UK case has been used as a model by numerous countries following in its path. The UK energy regulator, Ofgem, set the standard for qualified, independent regulators which are recognised as essential components of any competitive market. The UK was the first country to announce a major long-term carbon emission goal – 60% reduction by 2050 – and has been active in bringing climate change to the centre of global political discussions. The UK was also one of the first countries to develop a certificates obligation programme for renewable energy and is currently leading the way with a similar type of programme to support energy efficiency in the household sector. While there have been setbacks in some of these initiatives, the overall policy trend is a positive one. The government deserves credit for the fresh approach and new ideas it has brought to the energy sector.

The one overarching theme in these and other energy policy developments has been the use of the market to achieve policy goals. The UK is among those IEA countries that most rely on market actors, responses to price signals and private participation. Even when the government identifies a market failure (*e.g.* the negative externality of greenhouse gas emissions), it is quite likely to use a market-based instrument to correct it. This market approach has worked well for the UK and the government indicated it will continue with the same philosophy to meet future energy goals.

One of the primary challenges facing energy policy makers is energy security. This issue has numerous components based on several fundamental concerns, including: depletion of the country's oil and gas resources and resultant growing reliance on other countries to export to the UK; volatility in international energy markets – primarily crude oil; and ways to ensure the country does not suffer economically as a result. On the domestic front, energy security will require massive infrastructure investments in the next ten to fifteen years. The most pressing infrastructure need is natural gas import facilities in the form of subsea pipelines and liquefied natural gas (LNG) regasification terminals. Additional infrastructure investment will be needed to replace the coming wave of power plant retirements, primarily nuclear and coal-fired plants.

The 2006 UK Energy Review

In July 2006, the government released "The Energy Challenge," the first report from its Energy Review launched in late 2005. The visit of the IEA review team to London and the writing of this review took place prior to the release of the Energy Challenge and, thus, most of this book concerns policies in place prior to the UK Energy Review. However, we do provide a brief summary and assessment of the July 2006 report below and have changed the text of the book in those areas addressed or likely to be changed by the ongoing Energy Review.

Based on the July 2006 report – a more detailed White Paper is expected in the first half of 2007 – the Energy Review does not represent a major shift in approach or philosophy for the UK. Instead, it reinforces the UK's use of the market to meet energy goals. While details of some programmes are still to be released, no dramatically new policy tools will be introduced. Market forces and market tools – individual decision-making, prices set by supply and demand, and active trading between market participants – will continue to factor heavily in all energy policies.

The continued embrace of a market philosophy is shown in the following aspects of the review report.

For energy security, the government will:

- Promote more open and competitive international markets.

- Further develop a domestic market framework that is positive for investment and diversity of supplies and allows the private sector to make the necessary investment decisions.

- Remove barriers to nuclear power, but leave the private sector to initiate, fund, construct and operate nuclear plants, covering the full cost of decommissioning and waste storage.

- Create a framework to promote diversity, but leave the decision on how much gas the country uses to energy producers and consumers.

For GHG emissions reduction, the government will:

- Strengthen and expand the Renewables Obligation (RO), a market-based certificate trading scheme.

- Maintain an approach to energy savings that gives consumers more information and clearer incentives to make better use of energy, letting individuals take decisions.

- Consult on an emissions trading scheme for large non energy-intensive industries not covered by the EU-ETS and Climate Change Agreements.
- Work to develop the European Union Emissions Trading Scheme (EU-ETS) into a long-term international framework for pricing carbon.
- Press the European Commission to consider the inclusion of road transport and aviation in the EU-ETS.
- Have trials to determine the wider benefits of smart meters, testing their effectiveness in terms of reduced energy use and improved security of supply against cheaper options such as improved billing and real-time displays.

Although the IEA was unable to examine the details of the report, we would generally support its major tenets. In fact, many of the steps outlined in the Energy Challenge are consistent with the recommendations made in this in-depth review. Such shared conclusions include government plans to:

- Provide more certainty for market players on, among other areas, climate change, renewable energy and nuclear power.
- Look for ways to streamline the planning process for new energy infrastructure.
- Improve quality of energy-related data provided to the market.
- Provide framework for new nuclear plants and plan for dealing with legacy costs, but leave decision and financing of new nuclear plants to the private sector without subsidy.
- Expand energy-saving programmes to small and medium-sized enterprises (SMEs).
- Increase efforts to improve energy efficiency in the transport sector.

The natural gas supply problems in the winter of 2005/06 prompted some concerns about the market's ability to respond to tightening supply-demand balances in a timely fashion that avoids shortages. This report finds that the market is capable of providing adequate supply although the energy sector may occasionally face tighter supply-demand balances under a market-oriented system than under command-and-control. While such tightness will likely lead to temporary price spikes, the overall prices seen by consumers in the long run will be less in a market system. At the same time, trust in market mechanisms to provide energy supply in no way implies that the government has no role to play in energy security. The government must constantly monitor supply security and create an appropriate regulatory environment in which private players can act. Suggestions on further steps the government should take in this area are discussed below.

The winter 2005/06 represented an extraordinary series of events for the UK gas market: less domestic production, unutilised import capacity on the Belgium Interconnector and a fire at the Rough storage facility. Despite the combined effect of these events, there were no involuntary gas supply interruptions and the market continued to function well. In fact, it was the government's admirable restraint in not interfering with the market through price caps or other distortions that helped to spare the UK from shortages. Instead, high gas prices brought substantial demand reduction as users switched to other fuels or, more rarely, temporarily curtailed their gas-related activities. While colder temperatures would have further tested the system further, the demand response to high prices constituted an effective means of dealing with a highly unusual series of supply shortfalls.

The market also responded on the supply side with numerous initiatives for new infrastructure. Large investments in LNG regasification terminals, subsea gas pipelines, energy networks, domestic oil and gas production, and power plants are being planned to meet the country's energy infrastructure needs. While the majority will not be brought on line for several years, it appears that – despite sporadic delays in various projects – sufficient gas import infrastructure will be in place by the winter of 2006/07 to alleviate the supply tightness and price spikes of the winter, except in the event of extreme weather conditions. The government should continue to monitor these supply projects as well as the overall supply-demand balance for the winter of 2006/07.

- Although this report encourages the UK to maintain its core trust in the market as an important guarantor of energy security, there are still a number of steps the government should take to provide the proper framework:

- Provide as much certainty as possible for future policy directions.

- Improve availability and transparency of data on energy supply, demand and pricing.

- Allow demand to respond as much as possible to prices and/or supply tightness.

- Streamline the planning and consents process for new energy infrastructure.

Perhaps the primary action the government should take is to provide long-term clarity and certainty on policies affecting energy investments. This applies primarily to rules on GHG emissions, the treatment of nuclear power and long-term support for renewable energy. Uncertainty pushes investors to delay investment, which has important energy security implications. Providing policy certainty can be difficult, however. Government and political conditions are constantly evolving and over the lifetime of most energy infrastructure, these can be expected to change substantially. Nevertheless, there are steps the government should take to provide more guidance for future policy. These include being as transparent as possible in setting long-term energy goals and ensuring that all objectives and targets are pursued to the end with changes only if absolutely necessary. As many issues involve international co-operation, the UK government should continue to work with other countries to create clear investment conditions and frameworks such as the future framework of climate change mitigation post-2012.

The UK Energy Review has attempted to provide this certainty. The Renewables Obligation (RO) has been strengthened and very strong language in support of a post-2012 climate change framework is included. However, the nuclear sector has benefited the most from added clarity and certainty. In addition to giving the general signal that the government would not oppose new nuclear plants, specific proposals include:

- Setting out a framework for the consideration of issues relevant to planning and new nuclear plant construction.

- Providing the basis for long-term waste management.

- Developing guidance for potential promoters of new nuclear stations.

At present, these proposals are too vague to provide the required certainty and will need to be clarified – especially for the financing of decommissioning and waste storage. Further information is expected in the coming months or in the White Paper released at the turn of the year. However, the approach seen in the Energy Review report represents a positive start in providing clarity to investors on nuclear while still leaving the investment decisions to the private sector with no subsidies, guarantees or other explicit government support. The government is urged to provide more details on these proposals as soon as possible.

The second step the government should take is to improve wherever possible the availability of information. While the UK energy market has a high degree of transparency vis-à-vis other IEA countries, and a great deal of information is already available, more should be done in this area. Market players will not add supply if they do not have good information on which to make decisions. The UK government recognises the benefits that greater information can bring. One of the recommendations in the Energy Review is for the government to introduce new arrangements for the provision of forward-looking energy market information and analysis relating to security of supply. We encourage policy makers to follow through on this sound initiative.

In the natural gas sector, a great deal of information is available on the flows through the interconnector and from the United Kingdom Continental Shelf (UKCS) production. However, greater focus on predicting future production from the UKCS could be helpful. The Department of Trade and Industry (DTI) and the National Grid play an important role in assembling projections of future production from North Sea producers but they have no means to independently verify these projections. Further efforts to improve the quality of these projections would send signals to market participants about the coming need for gas supply infrastructure. In the electricity sector, three types of data could be made more readily apparent. The first would be the establishment of an actual market price of electricity. When the UK moved away from the electricity pool, policy makers expected that liquid forward markets would develop through commercial exchanges, including a day-ahead spot market. This has not materialised and, as a result, there is no clear market price that investors – particularly new entrants – can reference. The second way to improve information in the electricity sector is to extend the National Grid's electricity forecast. The current forecast of seven years is an excellent source of information to potential investors but it should be extended to ten years – matching the gas forecast – since many new power plants (*i.e.* possible nuclear or coal units) have development and lead times greater than seven years. The third area where more information would be helpful is real-time data on power plant operating status.

Information on the international energy sector would also be helpful. As the UK increases import dependence, knowledge of foreign activity will be increasingly important, especially in the natural gas sector. For example, problems from the winter of 2005/06 stemmed in part from actions taken on the continent and in Russia, together with the state of the global LNG market. The UK energy sector must adapt to the idea of greater interdependence with other countries and the government should play a role in facilitating that adaptation by providing relevant information on energy developments in other countries.

The third step the government should take is to create conditions where energy demand can respond to high prices. The winter of 2005/06 demonstrates how demand response is a key element to security of supply. The cost of supply infrastructure that meets demand under all scenarios is extremely high. While demand response is essentially a market decision taken by private consumers, the government has an important role in allowing that response to take place, particularly in addressing those market failures that dampen demand response.

A number of policy options are available in this area, the simplest probably being information campaigns. In periods of high prices and/or supply-demand tightness, the government should have a media campaign to alert people to the situation and encourage less energy use. The experience of the winter of 2005/06 – when many customers decreased demand even though their gas prices did not actually rise – shows how powerful public awareness can be. During the power shortfalls in California, media campaigns had even more profound effects. Another possibility includes more directly exposing consumers to changes in the wholesale market prices and giving them the information and ability to change their behaviour accordingly. The Office of Gas and Electricity Markets (Ofgem) is already working on smart meters and is encouraged to pursue this, especially in light of the cheaper smart meters currently being used. Another way to trigger greater demand response is by linking retail rates more closely to wholesale rates for both gas and electricity. Government work in this area poses some challenges since the contracts governing tariffs are private. However, the government should encourage a greater number of customers to pay tariffs linked real-time to wholesale markets. Another possibility involves dual fuel-firing at power plants and industrial facilities. A factory that switches from gas to fuel oil during high gas prices not only gives itself lower fuel costs, but also decreases the use of gas, a highly valued commodity, thus lowering prices and increasing availability for other users.

The fourth step the government should take is to streamline the process for infrastructure projects to obtain the necessary planning consents. Many potential investors in infrastructure have delayed or abandoned plans owing to difficulties with planning permits and consents. Such projects include gas storage facilities, LNG terminals and wind plants. Difficulties and delays in making such investments hamper the ability of the market to respond quickly to demand and thus jeopardise energy security. Local communities can and should have a degree of permitting authority for new facilities. However, since these facilities benefit the country as a whole, the UK government has a role in ensuring that permitting is not unduly delayed. The Energy Review also identifies planning as a major issue to be addressed. It describes the planning barriers facing new energy infrastructure and begins to develop a more effective, better co-ordinated planning process for such projects. While more needs to be done to flesh out and implement these ideas, we commend the government for addressing this issue and encourage it to move swiftly to resolve it.

Concerning the second major theme of this review – energy efficiency – the UK government places a very high emphasis on this area and plans to continue using energy efficiency as a major tool in achieving energy goals. The team commends the UK's focus on the demand side as a crucial component of a sound energy policy.

The government has implemented a wide range of energy efficiency policies and measures in the household, business and public sectors. While such a wide range of measures and programmes may lead to complications, dispersion of resources and occasional bureaucratic infighting, it also allows each programme to specialise in a particular area and to operate more independently and, ideally, more effectively. The government manages this inherent tension relatively well. The wide range of measures also makes comparing the cost-effectiveness of each measure more difficult, although the government has taken steps to address this problem through a Defra study released in April 2006.[1] Conclusions in the Defra study mirror analyses done in other countries, namely that efficiency and demand reduction measures generally offer more cost-effective solutions than supply-side measures. This validates the UK's focus on the demand side as a sound strategy. The government is encouraged to expand on such cost-effectiveness analysis and, more importantly, use it to determine the proper allocation of resources.

A major policy pillar in the household sector is the Energy Efficiency Commitment (EEC). Under the EEC, electricity and gas suppliers must achieve targets for demand reduction in the household sector by carrying out a combination of approved measures, including insulation, low-energy light bulbs, high-efficiency appliances and boilers. The programme's success can be attributed to various factors. First, putting obligations on a limited number of energy suppliers instead of numerous end-users has made system management relatively easy. Second, the regulator, Ofgem, publishes a list of pre-approved measures available to suppliers and how much energy savings each measure is worth. This simplifies the system and reduces administrative burdens for everybody. Third, there have been plenty of "low hanging fruit" for achieving the targets. Fourth, there have been various initiatives by the Energy Saving Trust involving consumers and manufacturers/retailers of energy-efficient equipments to supplement the EEC.

Despite its success, there are several challenges to be addressed in the EEC. First, given that low hanging fruit will be gradually exploited, broader measures such as microgeneration, behavioural changes and smart metering will need to be incorporated. At the same time, the government and Ofgem should ensure that such a wider scope will not result in unduly complicated and cumbersome administrative procedures. Of course, it is a challenge to broaden the scope while minimising administrative burdens. For this purpose, continuing the use of standardised and simple methodology for calculating energy savings from any newly introduced measure is essential.

In addition, the efficacy of incorporating social policy objectives in the EEC should be carefully evaluated. Currently, energy suppliers must realise at least half of their energy savings in the priority sector (*i.e.* low-income households). However, imposing such constraints likely reduces the overall cost-effectiveness of the system since attractive demand reduction in higher-income households may not be exploited. There is an equity issue to be considered. Since all consumers contribute equally to the cost of the EEC (through higher energy rates), supplier activity weighted towards upper-income customers would result in a subsidy from the less well-off to the better-off. However, EEC was launched as an energy efficiency programme and the 50% requirement hampers its

---

1. *Synthesis of Climate Change Policy Evaluations*, Department for Environment, Food and Rural Affairs (Defra), April 2006. Discussed more in Chapter 4.

ability to achieve its goals. While equity and fuel poverty are important issues, they can be pursued more effectively through more direct and targeted policies that are not incorporated in the EEC programme itself.

Improving the energy efficiency of large non energy-intensive industries and small and medium-sized enterprises (SMEs) is a challenge. The household sector has the EEC, as well as fuel poverty programmes for the disadvantaged, and the energy-intensive users have the Climate Change Levy (CCL), Climate Change Agreements (CCAs) and the EU-ETS, but there are fewer programmes for medium-size consumers. Increasing government efforts to fit energy users that fall between these two groups could be a cost-effective way to reduce demand. The Carbon Trust has proposed development of a new emissions trading scheme for large non energy-intensive industries and expansion of the EEC to SMEs. The Energy Review 2006 appears to favour the emissions trading option with the goal of reducing emissions by 1.2 MtC per year by 2020. The Review proposes an Energy Performance Commitment whereby some 5 000 organisations such as supermarket chains, hotel chains and government departments are required to participate in a trading scheme. Consultations and final decisions are expected during the first half of 2007. We caution the government to the complexity of such a trading scheme and encourage it to keep the minimum size of mandatory participants sufficiently large, so as not to unduly burden small companies that lack the resources and expertise to be active in such a scheme. The expansion of the EEC to SMEs should remain a possibility in the consultations. While this would also raise the administrative burden for participants and government, the success of the EEC in minimising such costs so far suggests that these challenges could be overcome. Another solution could be to expand the scope of CCAs to non energy-intensive industries and SMEs.

The government should do more to improve efficiency in the transport sector which has the highest rate of energy growth in the UK. While the government, largely through the Department of Transport, has a number of programmes to address transport energy demand, these efforts are not as substantial as those found in other sectors. In fact, efficiency transport measures at the Energy Savings Trust have recently been curtailed. The recent budget announcement that the vehicle excise duty (VED) will be further differentiated by vehicle efficiency is welcome but the sums involved remain minor and thus unlikely to have a great effect. For example, the introduction of a higher band of VED for the least efficient cars set at GBP 210 will only sway a small number of car buyers when considering the purchase of a vehicle that is already extremely expensive. In addition, shielding customers from high and/or volatile oil prices by deferring agreed, inflation-based tax increases – in effect lowering the real level of the tax – acts to increase transport demand at the exact time it should be reduced via a market response to price pressures.

The congestion charge in London is an innovative approach to traffic management. While not intended primarily as a means of curbing transport energy use, it does make operating a motor vehicle more costly and thus encourages environment-friendly travel such as public transport and bicycles. This provides a good example for other countries, a number of which are looking into similar programmes. While such congestion zones only make sense in large urban areas and their impact would be minimal on a national scale, the congestion zone nevertheless shows how transport projects aimed at easing traffic flow and improving the quality of life can, and normally do, also reduce energy demand. In this way, reducing transport demand should very much be a goal in all transport planning such as the the Department of Transport's (DfT) activities related to its 2004 White Paper, *Future of Transport: A Network for 2030.*

RECOMMENDATIONS

The government of the UK should:

General Energy Policy

▶ *Continue its stated and actual commitment to competitive energy markets as the primary tool for achieving energy policy goals while ensuring a clear and predictable framework for all market participants.*

▶ *Clearly define ways to achieve long-term emissions reduction targets in order to reduce uncertainty and to facilitate investments in supply infrastructure needed to ensure security of supply.*

▶ *Clarify further and provide more details on the investment framework for nuclear power, particularly in the treatment of nuclear waste and decommissioning for new and existing plants.*

▶ *Further improve the availability and quality of data on energy supply, demand and prices to better enable the market to meet security of supply objectives.*

▶ *Seek ways to accelerate planning and licensing procedures for new energy infrastructure.*

▶ *Continue to evaluate the long-term implications of the coming new wave of electricity generating stations in terms of both the effects of long-range carbon reduction objectives and potential over-reliance on certain fuels and technologies (i.e. gas-fired combined-cycle gas turbines).*

▶ *Ensure careful co-ordination between the various departments and authorities with responsibilities for energy and environment-related policy.*

▶ *Continue to take a proactive role in the full implementation of the EU internal energy market while at the same time considering the implications of possible delays in this process for the UK energy policy.*

Energy and Climate Change

▶ *Develop a clear and streamlined strategy to achieve its objective of reducing carbon emissions by 60% by 2050.*

▶ *Follow through and expand on analysis of the relative cost-effectiveness of the wide variety of measures brought forward in the Climate Change Programme 2006. Concentrate policies in sectors where emissions can be reduced the most and at the lowest cost.*

▶ *Carefully consider the ongoing use of multiple instruments (e.g. Climate Change Levy, EU Emissions Trading Scheme and Renewables Obligation) to reduce emissions from electricity generation.*

▶ *Avoid any overlaps in coverage between the Emissions Trading Scheme (ETS) and installations covered by Climate Change Agreements in phase 2 of the ETS.*

Energy Efficiency

▶ *Ensure that energy efficiency policies will be pursued not only from a climate change perspective but also from broader energy policy perspectives, including security of supply concerns, through close co-ordination between, the Department of Environment and that of Transport.*

▶ *Expand the cost-effectiveness analysis of energy efficiency policies and reflect the outcome in the portfolio of efficiency measures.*

▶ *Further improve the Energy Efficiency Commitment (EEC) by incorporating a wider range of measures, with the scope of promoting innovative energy efficiency technologies, while striving to simplify administrative procedures as much as possible through developing standardised methodology for calculating energy savings.*

▶ *Consider a tax incentive for households to supplement the effectiveness of the EEC.*

▶ *Reconsider the effect of ring-fencing 50% of EEC investment for priority groups on the overall cost-effectiveness of the programme and compare this with more direct and targeted measures to reduce fuel poverty.*

▶ *Examine experiences of White Certificate schemes in other countries and consider the feasibility of such a scheme in the UK.*

▶ *Increase predictability of future development of building codes, for example through advanced notice of proposed changes. Consider a time frame to incorporate the Code of Sustainable Homes in the building code.*

▶ *Improve enforcement of the building code by local authorities.*

- *Enhance the availability and quality of energy efficiency data in the household sector.*

- *Look for ways to fully include non energy-intensive industry and SMEs in the government's efficiency efforts, for example by expanding the EEC to allow suppliers to realise savings in the commercial sector, or by expanding the scope of Climate Change Agreements (CCAs).*

- *Take appropriate measures to capture energy efficiency potential in the sectors not covered by EU-ETS, CCA or EEC.*

- *Pursue additional means of curbing transport energy demand, and consider taxation, integration of demand concerns in a larger transport planning framework and other measures.*

Renewable Energy

- *Check for oversubsidisation of renewable energy technologies receiving high prices for Renewables Obligation Certificates (ROCs) and electricity prices as well as capital grants or other schemes.*

- *Look for lessons from other countries where renewables certificate schemes have achieved desired compliance rates at costs below current UK conditions.*

- *Examine more fully the costs and benefits of biofuels, including accurate assessments of carbon savings and benefits to national and global supply security coming from decreased oil demand.*

Electricity

- *Closely monitor the development of vertical integration of retail and generation in relation to the impact on competition and liquidity.*

- *Continue efforts to make fundamental information and analysis on supply and demand readily available to the market in order to ensure the investment environment is as transparent as possible.*

- *Consider ways to improve the framework for enhanced electricity market liquidity and enable the establishment of a strong reference price,* e.g. *through:*

  - *Working with the regulator Ofgem to adjust the pricing principles in the balancing mechanism with particular attention paid to the impact on the ability for new independent market players to take positions in the market.*

  - *Extending the locational signals, currently embedded in the network charges for generation, to traded electricity in the balancing mechanism in order to enhance transparency in the real-time wholesale pricing of electricity.*

Fossil Fuels

▶ Increase resources to provide reports on the crude oil and natural gas sectors, particularly on the likely future production, to provide the best possible signal to investors in the gas supply infrastructure.

▶ Ensure an upstream fiscal regime that stresses predictability in order to meet the twin goals of promoting investment and achieving a balance between oil producers and the country's interest.

▶ Examine the conditions required to encourage more natural gas storage, removing obstacles as much as possible, given the growing import dependence and the expected increase in gas-fired electricity generation.

Nuclear Energy

▶ Clarify the UK position regarding nuclear energy and, if applicable, establish a legal and regulatory framework for potential investors to assess with a reasonable degree of confidence the short- and long-term risks and benefits of building a new nuclear unit.

▶ Define a national policy covering the disposal of all types of radioactive waste and take steps towards its implementation to allow the industry to assess and fully internalise corresponding costs for existing and, if applicable, future nuclear power plants and fuel cycle facilities.

▶ Provide a robust and stable scheme for the accumulation, management and control of a fund for covering future financial liabilities (decommissioning and waste disposal) for existing and, if applicable, future nuclear power plants and fuel cycle facilities.

▶ Assess the adequacy of education and training for developing the human resources/qualified manpower needed to ensure the safe operation and decommissioning of existing nuclear units and, if applicable, the licensing and operation of new units.

Energy R&D

▶ Clearly define the government's role in the development and innovation of energy technologies with a view towards promoting a more active role in support of research, development, demonstration and deployment of energy technologies.

▶ Develop a strategy for energy RD&D consistent with energy policy goals.

▶ Consider an increase in the government budget for research and development to align it more closely with that of other IEA member countries.

- *Improve the oversight of public and privately funded RD&D (actors, funds, technologies) to enable the design of more cost-effective RD&D programmes and avoid overlap.*

- *Improve co-ordination between funding and priority-setting entities of public-funded energy RD&D programmes.*

- *Promote the role of the private sector in the definition and implementation of RD&D and continue to involve business in the design and targeting of public technology policy.*

- *Remain active in international collaboration to share technology development costs with other countries and to deal with problems that are essentially global, requiring significant funding over a long period of time.*

COUNTRY BACKGROUND

The United Kingdom of Great Britain and Northern Ireland (UK) is an island nation in Western Europe. The UK covers England, Wales, Scotland and Northern Ireland. The country shares a land boundary with only one country, the Republic of Ireland. The second closest country is France which lies 35 kilometres (km) at its closest point across the English Channel. The climate is temperate and moderated by the prevailing south-west winds related to the North Atlantic Current (also referred to as the Gulf Stream).

The UK population in 2006 was between 60 and 61 million inhabitants. The country has the fourth-highest population density of the 25 member countries of the European Union (EU) at approximately 245 people per square kilometre (km^2). The capital of London in the south-east of the country is by far the largest population centre. National population growth over the last 30 years has been approximately 0.2% annually.

The UK is a leading European and global trading partner and financial centre. Over the last two decades, the government has greatly reduced public ownership and contained the growth of social welfare programmes. The UK has substantial energy reserves, and production of oil, gas and coal accounts for around 10% of GDP, being among the highest share in industrialised nations. Services, especially banking and insurance, account for by far the largest share of economic activity while industry's share of GDP continues to decline. GDP growth slipped in 2001-2003 as the global downturn, the high value of the pound, and the bursting of the "new economy" bubble affected all sectors of the economy. Output recovered in 2004, with 3.2% growth, but moderated in 2005 to 1.7%. Although a member of the EU, the UK has opted not to join the Economic Monetary Union for the time being and thus retains the pound as its currency.

SUPPLY-DEMAND OVERVIEW

ENERGY SUPPLY

In 2004, the UK total primary energy supply (TPES) was 234 million tonnes of oil equivalent (Mtoe). (By way of comparison, in the same year, the US had a TPES of 2 326 Mtoe, Japan 533.2 Mtoe, Australia 116 Mtoe, Austria 33.2 Mtoe and France 275.2 Mtoe.) TPES in the UK grew by 0.6% from 2003 to 2004 and from 1994 to 2004 grew at annual average rate of 0.5%. By way of comparison, the average annual TPES growth for all OECD countries from 1994 to 2004 was 1.3%.

Natural gas and oil are the UK's dominant primary fuels, accounting in 2004 for 37.4% and 35.8% of TPES, respectively. These are followed by coal (16.0%), nuclear (8.9%), biomass (1.3%), hydropower (0.2%), wind and solar (0.1%), and imported electricity (0.3%). The major fuel supply trend of the last 30 years has been the rise in the share of natural gas at the expense of coal and oil. Oil use for electricity generation dropped from nearly one-quarter of the total to very small amounts today. Increased exploitation of substantial gas reserves in the UK Continental Shelf (UKCS) in the North Sea led to greatly expanded natural gas use, particularly in the 1990s when substantial gas-fired combined cycle gas turbine (CCGT) electricity generation was built. In recent years, coal supply has continued to fall while oil supply has stabilised and is now increasing, largely due to transport demand. Wind and solar have seen the greatest percentage growth, more than doubling from 2000 to 2004, although their combined overall contribution of 0.1% remains negligible. The government estimates that oil and gas will continue to be the dominant fuels up to 2020 and renewable energies will expand substantially but still only reach 1.2% of TPES in 2020.

Figure **1**

Total Primary Energy Supply, 1973 to 2020

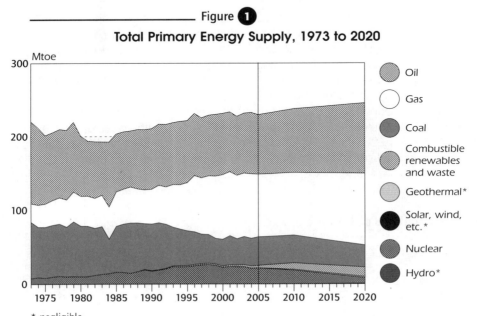

* negligible.
Sources: *Energy Balances of OECD Countries*, IEA/OECD Paris, 2006 and country submission.

Figure ❷

Total Primary Energy Supply in IEA Countries, 2005*

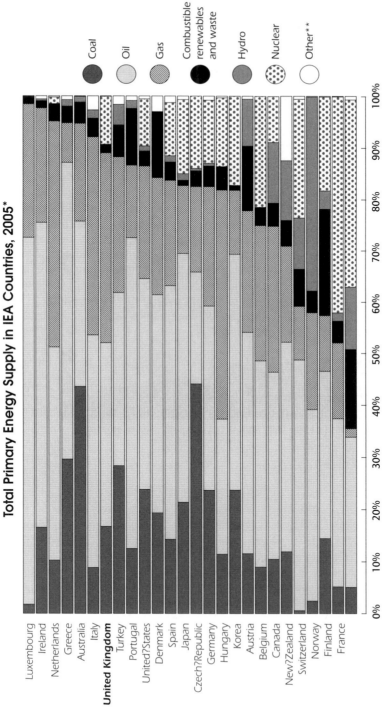

* preliminary data.
** includes geothermal, solar, wind, and ambient heat production.
Source: *Energy Balances of OECD Countries*, IEA/OECD Paris, 2006.

FOSSIL FUEL PRODUCTION

In 2004, the UK produced 99.6 Mtoe of oil, 86.4 Mtoe of natural gas and 14.9 Mtoe of coal. This production level made the UK the fifth-largest fossil fuel producer in the IEA (behind the United States, Canada, Australia and Norway). It was the third-largest gas producer and the fourth-largest oil producer among IEA members.

Figure **3**

Energy Production by Source, 1973 to 2005

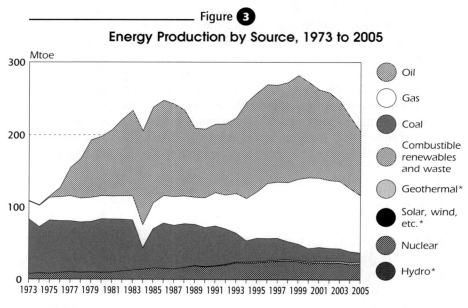

* negligible.
Source: *Energy Balances of OECD Countries*, IEA/OECD Paris, 2006.

Domestic coal production has been in decline for many years. Coal production peaked in 1913 with production approximately 12 times greater than it is today. Since the founding of the IEA in 1973, coal production has fallen by 80%. The phasing-out of government subsidies for coal in the mid- and late-1980s had a profound effect on the domestic mining industry. From 1988 to 1994, domestic production fell by 50%. Oil production reached a peak in 1999 when 143 Mtoe were extracted. From 1999 to 2004, however, production fell by 30% as the United Kingdom Continental Shelf (UKCS) fields matured. The production profile for gas is similar with peak production coming in 2000 (97.5 Mtoe) and falling by over 11% by 2004. Both oil and gas production fell further in 2005 but this information and further discussion can be found in Chapter 8.

ENERGY TRADE

The UK has been a net importer of fossil fuels in only six of the 24 years from 1980 to 2004. 2004 was the first year since 1991 that the country was a net fossil fuel importer. With the North Sea production falling and growing domestic demand, it is likely the UK will continue to be a net importer in the foreseeable future.

While the UK produced significantly more coal in the 1970s and early 1980s than it does today, it has not been a major exporting country. With the decrease in domestic mining activity since the late 1980s, imports have risen substantially, increasing by more than 160% from 1990 to 2004. In 2004, coal imports accounted for more than 60% of supply to the UK. 2004 was the first year since 1996 that the UK was a net natural gas importer. The decrease in production from the UKCS fields (and the consequent net imports) occurred more rapidly than expected. While oil remains a net export (15.3 Mtoe of net exports in 2004), declining production and increasing domestic demand will likely soon reverse this. (Discussion of oil and gas production and their effect on imports is explored more fully in Chapter 8.)

ENERGY DEMAND

In 2004, UK total final consumption (TFC) of energy was 163.7 Mtoe. From 1999 to 2003, TFC grew by an average annual rate of 0.4% and from 1973 to 2003, it grew by an annual average rate of 0.3% for a total increase of 11% over the 31 years. By way of comparison, TFC for the IEA as a whole rose by 31% from 1973 to 2003.

In 2004, oil was the most important energy source for final consumption, accounting for 47.2% of TFC. This was followed by natural gas (31.3%), electricity (17.9%), coal (1.9%), heat (1.2%) and biomass (0.3%) (see Figure 4 below). For the IEA as a whole in 2003, oil accounted for 52.7% of TFC, followed by gas (20.2%), electricity (19.6%), coal (3.2%), biomass (3.0%) and others (1.3%). The fuel whose share of TFC is substantially different in the UK than in the IEA as whole is natural gas. The higher share in the UK reflects the availability of North Sea domestic production and the extensive UK pipeline network.

The transport sector is the largest final energy user in the UK, accounting for 33.5% of TFC in 2004, 73% of which was used for road transport. The residential sector was the next largest user of energy with 27.4% of the total, followed by industry (20.0), other sectors (mostly commercial and public sector, 12.1%) and non-energy use (7.0%).

Figure 4

Total Final Consumption by Source, 1973 to 2020

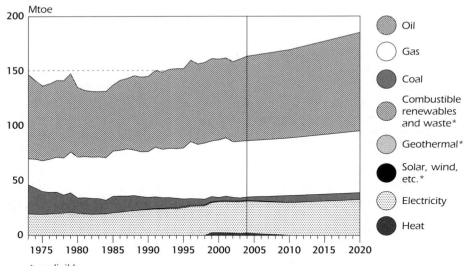

Legend:
- Oil
- Gas
- Coal
- Combustible renewables and waste*
- Geothermal*
- Solar, wind, etc.*
- Electricity
- Heat

* negligible.

Sources: *Energy Balances of OECD Countries*, IEA/OECD Paris, 2006 and country submission.

Figure 5

Total Final Consumption by Sector, 1973 to 2020

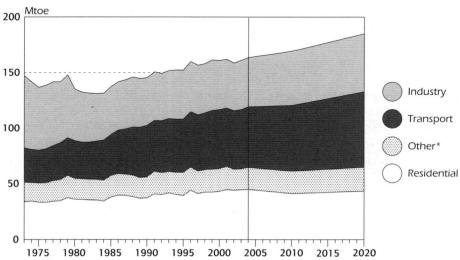

Legend:
- Industry
- Transport
- Other*
- Residential

* includes commercial, public service and agricultural sectors.

Sources: *Energy Balances of OECD Countries*, IEA/OECD Paris, 2006 and country submission.

GENERAL ENERGY POLICY

ENERGY POLICY OBJECTIVES

In July 2006, the government released *The Energy Challenge*, the first report from its Energy Review launched in late 2005. The visit of the IEA review team to London and the writing of the In-Depth Review took place prior to this document's release and, thus, most of this book concerns policies in place prior to the UK Energy Review. However, we do provide a brief summary and assessment of the July 2006 report in the Executive Summary and have changed the text of the book in those areas addressed or likely to be changed by the ongoing Energy Review.

In 2003, the government laid out its energy policy in an Energy White Paper[2] (EWP) published by the Department of Trade and Industry (DTI). The EWP recognised that the UK needed a new energy policy to address three key challenges:

● The threat of climate change.

● Dealing with the implications of reduced UK oil, gas and coal production and the likely consequent shift from being a net energy importer to being a net energy exporter.

● The need to replace or update much of the UK energy infrastructure in the coming 20 years.

To address these three challenges, the government set four goals for energy policy:

● Putting the country on a path to cut carbon emissions by some 60% by about 2050, with real progress by 2020.

● Maintaining the reliability of energy supplies.

● Promoting competitive markets in the UK and beyond.

● Ensuring that every home is adequately and affordably heated.

Regarding nuclear power, the White Paper of 2003 stated that "current economics make it an unattractive option for new carbon-free generating capacity, and there are also important issues of nuclear waste to be resolved." However, it explicitly did not rule out the possibility of new nuclear build as a necessary choice to meet the country's GHG emission targets. The EWP proposed no concrete policies that would either encourage or discourage new nuclear plants.

---

2. Available at www.dti.gov.uk/energy/whitepaper/index.shtml

The government continues to believe that the goals set out in the EWP provide the right framework for energy policy, and that they are achievable. As far as possible, the government ensures that the market framework and policy instruments reinforce each other to achieve their goals. The government recognises that inevitable tensions will arise among the goals. Its approach to alleviating these tensions or otherwise prioritise competing goals is guided by the following principles:

- Significant damaging climate change is an environmental limit that should not be breached.

- Reliable energy supplies are fundamental to the economy as a whole and to sustainable development. An adequate level of energy security must be ensured at all times in the short and longer term.

- Liberalised and competitive markets will continue to be a cornerstone of energy policy. Where the market alone does not, or cannot, create the right signals, the government will consider a range of interventions or measures that provide a framework for the markets to deliver the desired outcomes.

- The UK policies should take account of impacts on all sectors of society. Specific measures will be needed for particular groups of people (*e.g.* to support those for whom energy bills form a disproportionate burden).

The government keeps progress and policies under review, for example through the Climate Change Programme Review and the Renewables Obligation Review, both of which are ongoing. The government is also committed (in statute) to publishing an Annual Report on progress in implementing the EWP.[3]

On 29 November 2005, the Prime Minister announced a review of energy policy (the Review) to consider the UK's progress against the medium- and long-term EWP goals and the options for further steps to achieve them. The Review is assessing options on both the supply and demand side and is looking at the prospects for both existing and new low-carbon technologies, and for more aggressive uptake of energy efficiency measures. It is examining the potential contribution of carbon sequestration to allow continued use of the world's coal and other fossil fuel resources. It is also looking again at the role of nuclear electricity generation. On 23 January 2006, the government published a consultation document, *Our Energy Challenge: Securing clean, affordable energy for the long term*,[4] outlining in more detail the basis for the review, its assumptions, analysis and assessment of current trends and asking a series of questions.

---

3. The three reports already published are available at: http://www.dti.gov.uk/energy/policy-strategy/energy-white-paper/page21223.html

4. The document is available at: http://www.dti.gov.uk/energy/review/index.shtml

ENERGY POLICY INSTITUTIONS

DEPARTMENT OF TRADE AND INDUSTRY

The Department of Trade and Industry (DTI) has the primary responsibility for the development and implementation of UK energy policy on the supply side. The DTI's Energy Group deals with a wide range of energy-related matters, from production and generation to the eventual supply to customers. DTI's role is to set out a fair and effective framework in which competition can flourish for the benefit of customers, the industry and suppliers, and which will contribute to the achievement of the UK's environmental and social objectives.

DEPARTMENT FOR ENVIRONMENT, FOOD AND RURAL AFFAIRS

The mandate of the Department for Environment, Food and Rural Affairs (Defra) covers the interests of farmers and the countryside; the environment and the rural economy; UK food supply; and clean air and water. Within the energy sector, Defra is responsible for developing and implementing both the UK's policy on climate change and its policy on energy efficiency. Defra has lead responsibility for policies and measures to reduce energy demand in the UK.

THE OFFICE OF GAS AND ELECTRICITY MARKETS

The Office of Gas and Electricity Markets (Ofgem) is the UK regulator for electricity and natural gas. Its two primary goals are: *i)* to promote effective competition wherever appropriate, and *ii)* to regulate effectively the monopoly companies which run the gas pipes and the electricity wires. It also plays a role in facilitating discussion on energy matters by acting as both a forum and a participant in debates dealing with energy issues. Ofgem is funded by the energy companies that are licensed to run the gas and electricity infrastructure.

THE ENERGY SAVING TRUST AND THE CARBON TRUST

The Energy Saving Trust (EST) and the Carbon Trust (CT) are independent bodies funded by the government which promote energy savings and the reduction of carbon emissions. The CT is responsible for business and industry, while the EST deals with the general public. The CT delivers independent information and impartial advice on energy savings and carbon management and promotes government energy efficiency programmes. The CT also supports development of small-scale low-carbon technologies. The EST encourages energy efficiency and the integration of renewable energy sources into the economic fabric of UK society. To achieve this, it promotes the use of cleaner fuels for transport and better insulation and heating efficiency for buildings and homes and encourages small-scale renewable energy, such as solar and wind power.

ENERGYWATCH

Energywatch is an independent gas and electricity watchdog. It was set up in November 2000 through the Utility Act to protect and promote the interests of all gas and electricity consumers. This includes providing free and impartial advice, and even acting on behalf of consumers that feel they have been treated unfairly by their gas or electricity suppliers. Energywatch is funded by DTI through a licence fee paid by suppliers.

JOINT ENERGY SECURITY OF SUPPLY WORKING GROUP

In July 2001, DTI and Ofgem set up the Joint Energy Security of Supply (JESS) working group. JESS is jointly chaired by personnel from DTI and Ofgem, and brings together contributions from DTI, Ofgem, National Grid and the Foreign and Commonwealth Office (FCO). JESS is mandated to assess the risks to Britain's future gas and electricity supplies, to monitor the availability of gas and electricity supplies at least seven years in advance, and to determine whether market-based mechanisms are bringing forward timely investments. JESS must report twice yearly to the Secretary of State and the Gas and Electricity Market Authority, the body governing Ofgem.

DEPARTMENT FOR COMMUNITIES AND LOCAL GOVERNMENT

The Department for Communities and Local Government (DCLG) is the successor department to the Office of Deputy Prime Minister (ODPM). It has a remit to promote community cohesion and equality, as well as responsibility for housing, urban regeneration, planning and local government. For the energy sector, its responsibilities include building regulations and standards as well as planning for some energy infrastructure.

DEPARTMENT OF TRANSPORT

The Department of Transport's (DfT) objective is to oversee the operation and development of a reliable, safe and secure transport system that responds efficiently to the needs of individuals and business while safeguarding the environment. Its work in both individual and mass transit has important implications on UK energy demand. It is also active in the promotion of biofuels.

NUCLEAR DECOMMISSIONING AUTHORITY

The Nuclear Decommissioning Authority (NDA) is a non-departmental public body, set up in April 2005 under the Energy Act 2004 to take strategic responsibility for the UK's nuclear legacy. Its core objective is to ensure that the 20 civil public-sector nuclear sites under state ownership are decommissioned and cleaned up safely, securely, cost-effectively and in ways that protect the environment for this and future generations.

ENERGY RESEARCH PARTNERSHIP

The Energy Research Partnership (ERP) brings together top energy industry executives, government officials and senior academics in a Treasury-inspired initiative designed to give strategic direction to UK energy research, development, demonstration and deployment. The ERP, which also aims to help increase the level and impact of national R&D activity, was launched in January 2006. It operates alongside the UK Energy Research Centre (ERC), established in 2004.

ENERGY STATISTICS AND FORECASTS

DTI publishes a wide range of energy statistics, principally the Digest of UK Energy Statistics (DUKES) and the Energy Indicators. They post statistical information on their website on a monthly basis with an explanation of the methodology used to compile the data. These data are classified as National Statistics and are, therefore, produced to high professional standards and free from political interference, as set out in the National Statistics Code of Practice. The data undergo regular quality assurance reviews to ensure that they meet customer needs.

ENERGY FORECASTS

In February 2006, the DTI published the most recent energy and emissions forecast for the UK,[5] updating projections published in November 2004. These forecasts all assume that policy measures considered to be firm and funded (as of year-end 2005) are included, but that the potential impact of the European Emissions Trading Scheme (EU-ETS) is not included. The new forecast includes four scenarios with different fuel price projections:

- A high fossil fuel price case.

- A central fossil fuel price case, with prices slightly favouring natural gas over coal for power generation.

- A central fossil fuel price case, with prices slightly favouring coal over natural gas for power generation.

- A low fossil fuel price case.

All four scenarios make the same assumption on economic growth in the UK as shown in Table 1.

The assumptions on fossil fuel prices differ by scenario and are shown in Table 2.

Table **1**

Assumption on Economic Growth

	2006	2007	2008	2009-2020
Growth	2.25%	3%	3%	2.5%

5. *UK Energy and CO$_2$ Emissions Projections, Updated Projections to 2020*, DTI (February 2006).

_____ Table **2**

Assumptions on Fossil Fuel Prices

High fossil fuel price case

	Oil (USD/bbl)	Gas (pence/therm)	Coal (USD/GJ)
2005	60	36	2.60
2010	50	38	1.70
2015	50	38	1.70
2020	50	38	1.70

Central case favouring gas

	Oil (USD/bbl)	Gas (p/therm)	Coal (USD/GJ)
2005	55	36	2.50
2010	35	23	1.50
2015	35	23	1.43
2020	35	23	1.35

Central case favouring coal

	Oil (USD/bbl)	Gas (p/therm)	Coal (USD/GJ)
2005	55	36	2.50
2010	35	28	1.50
2015	35	28	1.43
2020	35	28	1.35

Low fossil fuel price case

	Oil (USD/bbl)	Gas (p/therm)	Coal (USD/GJ)
2005	50	36	2.40
2010	20	18	1.30
2015	20	18	1.15
2020	20	18	1.00

Source: *UK Energy and CO$_2$ Emissions Projections, Updated Projections to 2020*, DTI (February 2006).

RESULTS

Partial results of the four forecasts are shown below. They include primary energy supply separated by fuel (Table 3) and final end-use by consumers, separated by sector (Table 4). The forecasts of CO$_2$ emissions are included in Chapter 4.

_____ Table **3**

Forecasts of Energy Supply by Fuel (Mtoe)

Central case favouring gas

	2005	2010	2015	2020
Coal	39.4	34.9	32.4	23.3
Oil	75.3	78.2	81.5	83.8
Gas	94.4	94.2	103.2	112.8
Nuclear	18.2	18.0	8.3	6.4
Renewables	4.4	7.9	10.6	10.7
Electricity imports	0.9	1.0	1.1	1.1
Total	**232.5**	**234.2**	**237.1**	**238.2**

Central case favouring coal

	2005	2010	2015	2020
Coal	39.4	40.6	41.3	33.1
Oil	75.3	77.5	80.1	82.3
Gas	94.4	84.7	90.6	100.7
Nuclear	18.2	18.0	8.3	6.4
Renewables	4.4	7.9	10.6	10.7
Electricity imports	0.9	0.9	0.9	0.9
Total	**232.5**	**229.7**	**231.8**	**234.0**

Source: *UK Energy and CO$_2$ Emissions Projections, Updated Projections to 2020*, DTI (February 2006).

ENERGY TAXATION

The government's approach to energy taxation is outlined regularly through the Budget and Pre-Budget Reports[6] and within these reports, energy policy is addressed in chapters entitled "Protecting the Environment". The objective is sustainable growth through the integration of economic prosperity with environmental protection and social equity. The government uses a range of economic and other instruments, taking into account social and economic factors, including voluntary mechanisms, regulation, spending programmes, economic instruments and tradable permit systems.

_____

6. These are available on: http://www.hm-treasury.gov.uk/budget/budget_06/bud_bud06_index.cfm

Forecasts of Final Demand by Sector (Mtoe)

High fossil fuel price case

	2010	2015	2020
Transport	60.3	63.3	65.9
Residential	42.2	43.2	44.2
Industry	35.6	37.0	38.8
Services and agriculture	19.3	20.2	20.9
Total	**157.5**	**163.8**	**169.8**

Central case favouring gas

	2010	2015	2020
Transport	61.1	64.8	67.6
Residential	43.8	45.0	46.0
Industry	36.2	37.7	39.4
Services and agriculture	19.3	20.2	20.9
Total	**162.2**	**169.7**	**175.9**

Central case favouring coal

	2010	2015	2020
Transport	61.1	64.8	67.6
Residential	44.6	45.8	46.8
Industry	37.1	38.9	40.6
Services and agriculture	19.3	20.2	20.9
Total	**160.5**	**167.7**	**173.8**

Low fossil fuel price case

	2010	2015	2020
Transport	62.5	67.8	71.0
Residential	46.4	47.7	48.8
Industry	36.8	38.2	39.7
Services and agriculture	19.3	20.2	20.9
Total	**165.0**	**173.9**	**180.3**

Source: *UK Energy and CO_2 Emissions Projections, Updated Projections to 2020*, DTI (February 2006).

The framework for the use of economic instruments to meet environmental objectives was set out in 1997 in a *Statement of Intent on Environmental Taxation* and was subsequently developed further in *Tax and the Environment* published in 2002.

RECENT CHANGES

The government's Pre-Budget Report for 2006 (released in December 2005) announced an increase in the rate of supplementary corporation tax levied on UK offshore operators from 10% to 20%. This effectively increases the UK offshore ring-fenced corporation tax rate to 50%.

In the full Budget Report for 2006, the government announced a number of changes in energy-related taxes. The first concerned the Climate Change Levy (CCL). The CCL, introduced in 2001, was set up to encourage consumers to improve energy efficiency and reduce emissions of greenhouse gases (GHGs) through a price-based signal on energy usage. To support competitiveness, the introduction of the CCL was accompanied by a 0.3% point cut in employer national insurance contributions (NICs), which has led to a net reduction in tax liability for business. Rates of the levy are:

- 0.15p per kWh for gas.
- 1.17p per kg (equivalent to 0.15p per kWh) for coal.
- 0.96p per kg (equivalent to 0.07p per kWh) for liquefied petroleum gas (LPG).
- 0.43p per kWh for electricity.

The levy does not apply to fuels used by the domestic or transport sector, or fuels used for the production of other forms of energy (*e.g.* electricity generation). The 2006 Pre-Budget announced that the CCL would be increased with inflation as of 1 April 2007.

The 2006 Budget also announced reforms to vehicle excise duty (VED) in an effort to sharpen environmental incentives. These changes are:

- A higher band of graduated VED (band G), set at GBP 210[7] for petrol cars, will be introduced for the most polluting new cars (those above 225g of carbon dioxide emissions per kilometre).
- The VED rate for the small number of cars with the very lowest carbon emissions (band A) will be reduced to GBP 0 to encourage take-up and assist the development of the low-carbon car market.

---

7. On average in 2005, one GBP = USD 1.818.

- VED rates will also be reduced for band B by GBP 35 and C by GBP 5, frozen for bands D and E, and increased by GBP 25 for band F.

- Rates for pre-2001 registered cars and light goods vehicles in the lower band will be frozen with the higher band increased by GBP 5.

- The reduced rate of graduated VED for alternative-fuel cars will be extended to include those cars manufactured to run on high blend bioethanol (E85).

- In total, 50% of cars will see their VED frozen or reduced. Three million cars will pay VED of GBP 100 or less.

- Motorbike VED rates and the standard rate for post-2001 light goods vehicles (LGVs) will be increased in line with inflation (with VED for LGVs rounded to the nearest GBP 5), while heavy goods vehicles (HGVs) and bus VED will be frozen. All VED changes took effect from 23 March 2006.

In addition, the 2006 Budget had deferred the inflation-based increase in main road fuel duties until 1 September 2006. This deferral was in response to recently high and volatile prices in the oil and oil products markets.

SUFFICIENCY OF MARKET INVESTMENT FOR SECURE SUPPLY

INTRODUCTION

The UK has been a pioneer in liberalising energy markets and introducing competition. This development has shifted a great deal of energy supply activity from the public sector to the private sector. It has also freed consumers to select the energy supplier of their choice based on whatever criteria they choose (e.g. price, auxiliary services offered, environmental issues, etc.).

This liberalisation process (primarily in the gas and electricity sector) is generally regarded as successful by politicians, the energy supply industry and the public. There have been no major disruptions of energy, prices have gone down and more services are being offered. According to the DTI, domestic electricity prices fell in real terms every year from 1992 to 2003 with the exception of 1994 when an 8% value-added tax (VAT) was introduced. Over the same period (1992 to 2003), domestic gas prices also fell by more than 20% in real terms. Gas and electricity prices for industry fell even further than for households. In 2004 and 2005, the falling price trend reversed itself in both gas and electricity. This rise in recent years is treated in more detail below. Figure 6 shows a progression of price indices in real terms from 1990 to 2005.

Figure 6

Real Price Indices for Retail Energy, 1990 to 2005

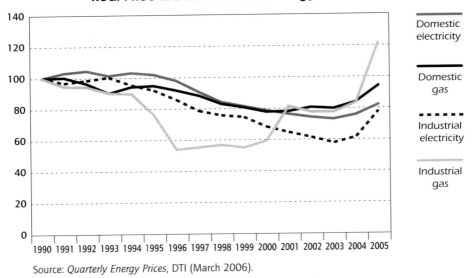

Domestic electricity

Domestic gas

Industrial electricity

Industrial gas

Source: *Quarterly Energy Prices*, DTI (March 2006).

SHIFTING RESPONSIBILITY FOR SECURITY OF SUPPLY

One aspect of the UK liberalisation is a decreasing role for the government. Previously, the government, through state-owned industry, was wholly responsible for providing secure, reliable gas and electricity supplies to all UK consumers. The government worked on the entire value chain from production to generation (for electricity), to transport, to final distribution of an end product to homes and businesses. It owned and operated and planned for all necessary infrastructure. The government also represented the demand side in explicit demand-side management programmes intended to curb demand.

With the move to competition, the government's role in ensuring supply security has decreased. In a market with perfect theoretical competition, government would play no role. In such a world, the market – both supply and demand – would value energy supplies and the degree of security of those supplies. Different consumers would pay for different levels of supply reliability based on their individual needs. Suppliers, motivated solely by profit considerations, would respond to these price signals and offer supplies and services that match the consumers' needs. In reality, however, there are a number of factors which make energy different from other markets and which call for a continuing government role in security of energy supply. These factors include:

- Energy supply has historically been guaranteed by the government and many still view it as a public good rather than a consumer product or a commodity.

- Energy supply investments are often very large and long-term, thus carrying substantial risk that can deter private investment.

- Energy, particularly electricity, is difficult and costly to store. This, coupled with unpredictable demand which varies hourly, daily and seasonally, makes serving the peak demand under all contingencies unprofitable and/or extremely costly.

- The success of infrastructure investments rests to a degree on government policy decisions and international geopolitical events, both of which can be difficult to predict and thus can deter private investment.

- Thus, government still plays a role in security of supply but the exact nature and scope of that role is no longer as clear as it once was.

HISTORICAL AND FUTURE INFRASTRUCTURE REQUIREMENTS

Since the liberalisation of the gas and electricity sectors, the UK has not had problems with reliability of supply. Sufficient infrastructure has been in place to meet demand. For example, in the electricity sector, the reserve margin has never fallen below 25%. It was 35% in 1990, fell to a low of 25% in 1993 and by 2004 had risen to 33%. From 1990 to 2004, installed capacity rose by more than 10% and now includes nearly 27 GW of combined-cycle gas turbine (CCGT) plants built since the introduction of competition. The CCGT investments alone are roughly equal to USD 16 billion.[8] In the natural gas sector, sufficient private-sector infrastructure investments were made to allow domestic production to expand from 40.9 Mtoe in 1990 to 86.4 Mtoe in 2004, an increase of 111%.

There were a number of factors at the outset of liberalisation not directly related to the liberalised market or competition that partly shaped the market response:

- There legacy of overcapacity in the electricity sector from the regulated period and much of this was based on previously subsidised coal-fired generation.

---

8. Assuming USD 600/kW for installed cost of CCGTs and total new CCGT build of 26.57 GW = USD 15.9 billion of required investment.

- Discoveries and production of oil and gas in the UKCS.

- An improved technology – CCGT power plants – in combination with North Sea gas created an incentive to build new generating stations to replace older coal-fired plants that had become highly politicised.

The current situation in the UK is marked by an expected need for massive infrastructure investments to meet future demand. In the electricity sector, a substantial portion of the generation fleet – primarily the large coal and nuclear plants – will reach the end of their nominal lifetimes in the next ten years. In the natural gas sector, continuing depletion of North Sea fields will require greater imports and the physical infrastructure to make those imports.

The National Grid produces reports every year which project likely energy infrastructure needs seven years into the future for the electricity market and ten years into the future for the gas market. These reports are discussed in more detail in Chapters 7 and 8. By way of summary, the National Grid ten-year gas statement predicts that gas demand will grow by 2.2% per annum through 2014 with peak demand growing by 2.1% per annum. Combined with depletion of domestic gas production, this will lead to a massive increase in import dependence. From the current modest levels, import dependence will rise to 52% in 2011/12 and then to 81% in 2014/15. Thus, massive import infrastructure in the form of LNG regasification facilities and subsea pipelines will have to be developed and built in the next ten years.

National Grid's seven-year forecast for electricity projects that there will be a gross increase in generating stations from new build equal to 14.1 GW between 2005/06 and 2011/12. Of this amount, the largest shares will be CCGTs (6.5 GW) and wind power (5.5 GW). Substantial additional generation will be needed in the years following the end of the National Grid's forecast period. In the eight years from 2011 to 2019, nearly 6 GW of nuclear capacity will be decommissioned (based on published lifetimes of the plants). Many coal plants will also be facing retirement around the same time. For the electricity transmission system, the seven-year forecast notes that there are some existing bottlenecks in the system and that these are projected to become more severe with the development of additional wind power in the north of the country and thus increase north-to-south electricity flows.

Planned Infrastructure Investments

A number of new infrastructure additions are currently being planned, or are already under construction. Information on announced investments is listed below by category.

Gas import and storage infrastructure

In May 2006, the Secretary of State for Trade and Industry announced that he had identified more than GBP 10 billion of planned and actual investments in gas import infrastructure, storage and related transportation between 2005 and 2010. He estimated that this could more than double the UK gas storage capacity and more than triple the import infrastructure.

In its ten-year statement on expected infrastructure needs, the National Grid identifies 11 import-related investments either planned or taking place. All would be operational by 2010. These include four pipelines (or pipeline additions) which will bring an additional capacity of 58.4 billion cubic metres (bcm) per annum. There are also seven LNG facilities with a combined capacity of 60 bcm. This added capacity of 118.4 bcm (if fully realised) is nearly the same as the expected total demand for the UK in 2010 (117 bcm).[9] The National Grid projects that the UK domestic production will still be able to meet more than half of the domestic demand and thus planned investments could provide twice the necessary import infrastructure needed by 2010, which would come in addition to existing infrastructure.

The National Grid currently identifies 11 gas storage projects currently in some stage of construction or development. They are all planned to come on line by 2010 and, if fully realised, would bring a total additional storage capacity of 5 700 million cubic metres (mcm). This would more than double the existing storage capacity of 3 759 mcm.

In addition to gas import infrastructure investments, at least one company is planning to expand coal import facilities. A GBP 10 million port expansion has been announced for the Port of Tyne to accommodate a greater flow of coal imports.

Generating stations

While low wholesale power prices and comfortable reserve margins have in the past few years deterred new investments in generation, a recent upturn in prices and the looming retirement of much of the UK fleet has led to some interest in generation investments. A number of companies have announced plans to build new generating stations in the UK. These include Centrica's announced plan for a 885-MW CCGT to be built at Langage (on line by 2008/09); RWE npower's announced plan for a 1-GW coal plant at Tilbury in Essex (on line by 2016); E.On UK's announced plan for a 450-MW integrated gasification combined cycle (IGCC) power station in Lincolnshire; and Scottish

---

9. Of course, demand is highly seasonal in the UK and thus the sufficiency of import infrastructure must take into account meeting winter peak demand which would also depend on storage capability.

and Southern Energy's announced plan for a 500-MW coal-fired plant at Ferrybridge. In addition, a number of other private-sector IGCC projects have been announced. All these coals plants would have the capability to integrate carbon capture and storage (CCS) technology at a later date.

Large investments are also planned for renewable energy generation. To meet the targets under the Renewables Obligation (RO), many renewable energy plants (primarily wind) are being developed and constructed. High prices for both electricity and renewables generation are attracting investments although construction and plant completion has been delayed at times by difficulties obtaining permits and planning permission.

In addition, a number of companies are said to be weighing the prospect of building new nuclear plants. However, these companies claim they seek certainty with regard to the government's position on nuclear and a clear message on what their obligations would be regarding nuclear waste disposal and decommissioning.

Electricity and gas networks

Substantial new investment is being planned to upgrade the high-voltage electricity transmission grid and the high-pressure gas pipeline network. The regulator, Ofgem, announced in June 2006 that it proposed twice the capital expenditure in the coming price control period (2007–2012) than in the previous period. Ofgem noted that energy networks face "huge challenges" over the next five years to respond to changes in the sources of gas and power. These changes primarily refer to an expected increase in wind farms in remote areas and higher volumes from LNG imports.

In total, Ofgem proposed GBP 5 billion in network capital spending for the 2007 to 2011 period. This would mean GBP 737 million for National Grid Gas, GBP 2.8 billion for National Grid Electricity Transmission, GBP 555 million for Scottish Power Transmission and GBP 164 million for Scottish Hydro-Electric Transmission. A supplementary GBP 750 million could be used as additional investment for potential new projects.

Offshore Oil and Gas Production

The gas and oil fields on the UKCS are mature and many are starting to decline. While there have been some substantial new discoveries recently (*e.g.* the Buzzard field) and exploration continues, the government and industry expect production in this area to decline steadily over time. Nevertheless, high gas and oil prices have led to renewed activity in the UKCS. A survey by the UK Offshore Operators Association (UKOOA) showed expenditures in the UKCS were rising. Total capital expenditure (excluding exploration, appraisal and decommissioning) rose from a level of GBP 3.3 billion in 2004 to GBP 4.4 billion in 2005 and, according to industry surveys, will rise to GBP 4.8 billion in 2006.[10] When analyst and service company Fugro Robertson recently surveyed 200 production companies to rate their interest in new ventures in 152 different countries, the UK ranked as the fourth-most attractive.

The Impact of Uncertainty on Energy Infrastructure Investments

The large infrastructure investments needed to maintain UK energy security require a market environment attractive to investors. One important aspect of this is the energy price, but another is certainty, or stability, of the investment climate. One of the major uncertainties in the energy sector is climate change or, more specifically, polices that will be enacted to curb emissions causing climate change.

A recent IEA report, *Impact of Climate Change Uncertainty in Power Investment*, looks at the effect that this uncertainty has on energy investments, primarily for power generating stations. Using the theory of real options, the report estimates both the value of waiting to make an investment when facing uncertainty and how different degrees of uncertainty will affect the choice of technology (*i.e.* coal-fired vs. CCGT plants).

While this work is still ongoing, some preliminary conclusions are:

- Climate change policy uncertainty can alter the investment case for new generation. Carbon prices may need to be substantially higher than expected under a normal discounted cash-flow analysis to justify a low-carbon technology in the face of uncertainty. In addition, electricity prices may need to be higher than expected to encourage investment in traditional (gas and coal) power generation.

- Free allocation of emission allowances to new entrants significantly alters the investment case. If it is done on the basis of providing a fixed percentage of a plant's expected emission allowances, then freely allocated allowances would be worth almost twice as much for coal plant as for gas plant.

- Changing from a 5-year to a 10-year trading/allocation period could significantly reduce the investment thresholds in the early years of the allocation period.

- The ability to retrofit carbon capture and storage (CCS) at a later date acts as a good hedge for coal plant against higher than expected carbon prices. The presence of CCS as a retrofit option makes new coal plant less risky (reducing the investment threshold in the face of uncertainty), and could accelerate investment in coal.

---

10. This survey took place prior to the increase in the supplementary corporate tax on UK offshore operators from 10% to 20% which may act to deter investment activity.

SHORT-TERM SUPPLY TIGHTNESS

While the UK has enjoyed low energy prices and sufficient levels of energy infrastructure with comfortable reserve margins over the last 10 to 15 years, it has recently seen substantial price rises for gas and electricity and a general tightening of the supply-demand balance. On the basis of DTI price data, the retail price for electricity rose by 16% in real terms during the two years from Q4 2003 to Q4 2005. The gas price rose by 24% over the same time. For industrial customers, retail electricity prices rose by 58% (in real terms including CCL) from Q4 2003 to Q4 2005 while gas prices rose by 93% (in real terms including CCL).

Chapter 8 includes a full description of the market tightness in the gas market during the winter of 2005/06. In short, it was caused by less supply than expected. While the temperatures were slightly colder than normal – 0.4°C below the average for the months November 2005 through March 2006 – this did not precipitate a demand rise to cause the tightness. Instead, it came from three developments that curtailed supply: i) supply from the UKCS was less than had been predicted by government and industry; ii) gas flow from the continent via the subsea interconnector with Belgium was below capacity despite substantially higher UK prices; and iii) there was a fire at the Rough storage facility in February 2006. These events led directly to higher gas prices, and also had a secondary effect on the electricity market where the marginal plant setting the price is very often fired by natural gas.

The high energy prices seen at the wholesale and retail levels prompted substantial changes in demand behaviour, compared to the forecast and demand in previous years. A National Grid report from May of 2006[11] estimated this level of demand response from gas consumers by comparing observed demand to forecasts. Over the top 100 demand days for the winter of 2005/06, the average level of demand response from daily metered customers was around 27 mcm per day. This represents more than 6% of the highest daily demand of 411 mcm per day. In addition to demand response from daily metered consumers, the National Grid report estimates that non-daily metered demand was typically 3% to 4% lower than had been forecast. Table 5 below describes the demand response in greater detail.

DTI also reported on changes in gas use in 2005 compared to 2004. In 2005, residential gas use rose by 1% while it fell by 3.2% in the industrial sector and by 5.7% for power generators. This does not include most of the winter 2005/06 when higher prices had a further effect on demand.

---

11. *Winter 2006/07 Consultation Document*, National Grid (May 2006).

_____ Table **5**

Demand Response to High Gas Prices, Winter 2005/06

Sector	Comment
NTS Power Stations [1]	Contributed the majority of the demand response: around 20 mcm/day on average and up to 40 mcm/day when the gas price was at its highest
NTS Industrial Loads	Around 3-4 mcm/day when the gas price was at its highest
LDZ Daily Metered Interruptible [1]	Around 5-10 mcm/day when the price was at its highest
LDZ Daily Metered Firm	Around 2 mcm/day when gas prices spiked in March
LDZ Non-daily metered	Demand estimates to have been depressed 3-4%

1. "NTS" refers to the national gas transport system and "LDZ" refers to local distribution zones.
Source: *Winter 2006/07 Consultation Document*, National Grid (May 2006).

The same National Grid document looked at likely import infrastructure projects expected to be ready by next winter's gas demand season, and all of them were completed by early December 2006. These are the Langeled pipelines from Norway to Easington (25 bcm or 68 mcm per day), the upgrade of the Belgium Interconnector (7 bcm or 19 mcm per day), the BBL pipelines linking the UK market with the Netherlands (16 bcm or 44 mcm per day) and the Excelerate floating LNG regasification facility at Teesside (4 bcm or 11 mcm per day). Taken together, they offer an additional import capability of 52 bcm per annum, or 142 mcm per day. As mentioned above, the maximum demand seen in the winter of 2005/06 was 411 mcm per day.

CRITIQUE

UK energy policy of the last ten years has been rather successful. The country has had secure energy at low prices and has taken important steps towards addressing GHG emissions on both domestic and international levels. Its pioneering work in market liberalisation of the gas and electricity sectors has brought many benefits and provided a good example for other countries. The strong UK commitment to competitive energy markets has resulted in clear benefits for UK energy consumers and a diverse energy sector.

This commitment to markets was tested in the winter of 2005/06 when lower-than-expected domestic gas production and imports led to very high prices and the threat of supply disruptions. The experience led to questions about the UK's energy supply security. More generally, discussions began on the ability of such a market-oriented system to provide secure supply or whether the government should play a larger role.

This report finds that the events of the winter 2005/06 do not constitute an argument against the market's ability to provide for security of supply. The three factors curtailing supply – less domestic production, unused import capacity on the Belgium Interconnector and the fire at the Rough storage facility – represented an extraordinary confluence of events. On top of that, winter temperatures were lower than the average, albeit just slightly, which would normally raise demand. Despite the combined effect of these events, there were no involuntarily interruptions in the gas supply. Had there been significantly colder temperatures, however, the system would have been much more constrained and, in this sense, the country was fortunate.

The market's ability to handle the lower-than-expected gas supply rested on two factors. One, the government did not intercede to cap prices or otherwise interfere with market dynamics. During similar energy supply-demand tightness seen in other markets – for example, the electricity markets of Ontario, Canada and Victoria, Australia – governments have limited the market prices for energy which actually exacerbated the situation. The UK government should be commended for its hands-off treatment of the gas market and its commitment to the functioning of the market.

The second factor helping the gas market get through the winter of 2005/06 was demand response in the face of high prices. According to the National Grid, the average demand response from the daily metered customers for the top-100 demand days was more than 6% of the highest daily demand throughout this period. Therefore, for an average day, overall demand was less and thus the demand response to prices was a greater percentage of the total. In addition, customers without daily metering also reduced demand from expected levels by between 3% and 4%. This is somewhat unexpected since these customers were not directly exposed to market prices and most likely lowered demand owing to media coverage of the high wholesale gas prices. The magnitude and scope of this demand response demonstrates an important tool in ensuring security of supply, even in the event of supply curtailment.

To give a longer-term perspective on the UK market's ability to respond to changes while still ensuring security of supply, this report considers the major development seen in the country in the 1990s: the so-called "dash-for–gas". The beginning of the decade saw the introduction of a cheaper, reliable fuel in North Sea gas, an upcoming technology in CCGT plants and a legacy of coal mining and coal-fired power stations that had become highly politicised. The logical path at that point was to exploit North Sea gas and use it to substantially alter the generating fleet by replacing coal-fired plants with gas-fired CCGTs. This opportunity for change coincided with the introduction of market dynamics in the UK energy sector. Driven by competition and profit motives, market players successfully realised this major shift from coal to gas. This occurred in a remarkably short period of time, brought lower prices for consumers and never jeopardised the country's energy security. It is impossible to say whether this transition could have occurred under a command-and-control economic model, but it is clear that the market's role in facilitating this paradigm shift was highly successful.

The major challenge now facing the UK energy sector is the massive construction of infrastructure to provide for the import of natural gas and to replace a substantial share of the generating fleet that will be retired in the coming 10 to 15 years. While the market successfully handled both the short-term gas tightness in the winter of 2005/06 and the transition to gas in the 1990s, this report concludes that it is still the best option to meet this major challenge and thus provide for supply security, and encourages the UK government to continue with its core philosophy allowing the market to determine the supply and demand profiles for all fuels. The one exception to this approach concerns geopolitical concerns. The government still has a strong role to ensure that the country's energy security will not be jeopardised by geopolitical concerns, by providing a secure long-term framework for investors in infrastructure.

The market is already responding on the supply side with numerous developments for new infrastructure. High prices are having their effect. Investments in LNG regasification terminals, subsea gas pipelines, energy networks, UKCS oil and gas production and power plants are being planned to meet the country's energy infrastructure needs. While the majority of this will not be brought on line for several years, it appears that sufficient gas import infrastructure will be in place by the winter of 2006/07 to avoid the supply tightness and high prices of the previous winter.

While this report encourages the government to maintain its core trust in the market providing supply security, there are nevertheless a number of steps to take to provide the proper framework for this to occur. This report identifies four sets of actions the government should pursue to best allow the market to provide for UK energy security:

- Providing as much certainty as possible for future policy directions.

- Making data on energy supply, demand and pricing available.

- Allowing demand to respond as much as possible to high prices and/or supply tightness.

- Streamlining the planning and consents process for new energy infrastructure.

Perhaps the primary action for the government is to provide long-term clarity and certainty on policies affecting energy investments. This applies primarily to rules on GHG emissions but would also include treatment of nuclear power and the long-term support for renewable energy. Uncertainty over future policies pushes investors to delay investment or to abandon it altogether as too risky. This has important energy security implications. Policy uncertainty also influences the kind of investment likely to be made. In the electricity market, uncertainties favour CCGT technology because: *i)* they can be built more quickly than other plants, thus reducing the chance of a policy change before revenue-generating plant operation begins, *ii)* their upfront cost are lower than those of other generation technologies, and *iii)* they emit less CO_2 and thus have less exposure to changes in carbon prices. However, too many CCGTs will lead to a higher dependence on one fuel and thus – even if built on time to meet demand – will have energy security implications.

Providing policy certainty can be difficult, however. Government and political conditions are constantly changing and over the lifetime of most energy infrastructure, these can be expected to change substantially. In addition, many of the issues where certainty is required involve international negotiations which no one government can directly control. Nevertheless, there are steps the government should take to give greater comfort over future policy directions. The government should be as transparent as possible about its long-term wishes for the energy sector. It should also ensure that any long-term statements and targets are, in fact, pursued. The likely failure in meeting the UK's 2010 CO_2 emissions target diminishes the government's credibility and undermines certainty. More concrete activity towards the 2050 goal of a 60% emissions reduction could restore some certainty. The government should be very reluctant to change policy approaches unless absolutely necessary.

The UK Energy Review has attempted to provide this certainty. The Renewables Obligation has been strengthened and very strong language in support of a post-2012 climate change framework has been included. However, it is the nuclear sector that has benefited the most from added clarity and certainty. In addition to giving the general signal that the government would not oppose new nuclear plants, specific proposals include:

- Setting out a framework for the consideration of issues relevant to planning and new nuclear build.

- Providing the basis for long-term waste management.

- Developing guidance for potential promoters of new nuclear stations.

At present, these proposals are too vague to provide the required certainty and will need to be fleshed out – especially for the financing of decommissioning and waste storage. Further information is expected in the coming months or in the White Paper released at the turn of the year. However, the approach seen in the Energy Review report represents a positive start in providing clarity to investors on nuclear while still leaving the investment decisions to the private sector with no subsidies, guarantees or other explicit government support. The government is urged to provide more details on these proposals as soon as possible.

At the same time, the government will never be able to fully eliminate policy uncertainty in any area of the energy sector and thus, there will never be a perfect security for investors. The government must be aware of how this uncertainty affects market players and adjust its policy accordingly. For example, as noted above, uncertainty favours CCGTs over other technologies but too many CCGTs pose a security threat because they diminish diversity of fuels and sources for fuels. Thus, in this instance, the government must monitor how the inherent policy uncertainty affects the market and, in the event that the market responds with excessive dependence on a single supply option, take steps to see diversity is maintained, by taking appropriate measures to assure investors in other supply options about the potential return on their investment.

The second step the government should take is to improve wherever possible the availability of information. While the UK energy market has a high degree of transparency *vis-à-vis* other IEA countries, and a great deal of information is already available, more could and should be done in this area. Investors can only make decisions on the basis of available price and supply/demand data and the government is uniquely positioned to provide these data and/or ensure that market participants make the data public.

In the natural gas sector, a great deal of information is available on the flows through the interconnector and from UKCS production. However, greater focus on accurately predicting future production from the UKCS could be helpful. One reason for gas market tightness in 2005/06 was actual production less than that forecast by DTI. DTI plays an important role in assembling production forecasts received from individual North Sea producers, in aggregating the results and making them public. However, it does not have the means to independently verify these projections and producers can have a variety of motivations to provide forecasts that may not be borne out. Further efforts to improve the accuracy of these forecasts would go a long way in sending signals to market participants about the coming need for a gas supply infrastructure.

In the electricity sector, two types of data could be made more readily apparent. The first involves the actual market price of electricity. Most liberalised electricity markets operate power exchanges or pools which produce a clear electricity price as supply and demand offers are matched up. When the UK moved away from the pool, policy makers expected various liquid forward markets would develop through commercial exchanges, including a day-ahead spot market. This has not materialised. The current level of forward trading is not very liquid and transparent, and a spot market setting a strong reference price has not emerged. In addition, the system is also lacking transparent locational pricing since transmission congestion is managed through re-dispatch. The increased transparency from nodal or zonal prices has helped boost liquidity in many other voluntary spot markets in other countries. The government is encouraged to develop a framework where a clear market price develops and where liquid futures markets give some indication of coming price trends. The other area where greater transparency would be helpful is real-time information on power plant operating status. A continuous flow of information about supply and demand fundamentals, including appropriate real-time information on generation plants, is crucial for an effective market.

The National Grid's forecast for both electricity and gas provide an excellent source of information to potential investors. This should certainly be continued and any additional resources allocated to this task as necessary. This report encourages the National Grid to extend its electricity statement to ten years – matching the gas outlook – since many new power plants (*i.e.* possible nuclear or coal units) have development and lead times greater than seven years.

Information on the international energy sector would also be helpful. As the UK increases import dependence, knowledge of foreign activity will be increasingly important, especially in the natural gas sector. For example, problems from the winter of 2005/06 stemmed in part from actions taken on the continent, actions taken in Russia and the state of the global LNG market. The UK energy sector must adapt to the idea of greater interdependence with other countries and the government should play a role in facilitating that adaptation by providing relevant information on energy developments in other countries.

The third step the government should take is to create the conditions where energy demand can respond to high prices. The winter of 2005/06 demonstrates how demand response is a key element to security of supply. The cost of a supply infrastructure that meets demand under all scenarios is extremely high. The price of supplying those final units of energy is much greater than the economic cost of that energy not being available. While demand response is essentially a market decision taken by private consumers, the government has an important role in allowing that response to take place. The government is encouraged to investigate this area and take all steps necessary to encourage demand response. A range of policies to achieve demand reaction in case of a supply crisis in the electricity sector were outlined in the IEA publication *Saving Electricity in a Hurry*, published in 2005, and some of these which are appropriate to the UK are outlined below.

The simplest is probably information campaigns. In periods of high prices and/or supply-demand tightness, the government should have a media campaign to alert people to the situation and encourage less energy use.

The experience of this past winter, when non-daily metered consumers not directly exposed to gas price rises decreased their consumption by 3% to 4% only thanks to media reports without any concerted government efforts shows how powerful public awareness can be. During the power shortfalls in California, media campaigns encouraging less power use had even more profound effects.

Another possibility includes more directly exposing consumers to changes in the wholesale market prices and giving them the information and ability to change behaviour accordingly. Ofgem is already doing work on smart meters and is encouraged to pursue this, especially in light of the cheaper meters currently available. Another way to trigger greater demand response is by linking retail rates more closely to wholesale rates for both gas and electricity. Government work in this area poses some challenges since the contracts governing tariffs are private. However, the government should do what it can to encourage a greater number of customers to pay tariffs linked real-time to wholesale markets.

Another possibility involves dual-fuel firing at power plants and industrial facilities. For example, a factory switching from gas to fuel oil during high gas prices not only benefits directly from lower fuel costs but also decreases its use of a highly valued commodity (gas), thereby lowering the price and increasing availability of the commodity for other uses. Thus, fuel-switching presents benefits for the economy as a whole and justifies a possible government role.

A more fundamental step the government should take is to streamline the process for infrastructure projects to obtain the necessary planning consents. Many potential infrastructure investors described how their plans were delayed or abandoned altogether because of difficulties in obtaining local planning permits and other consents. This includes gas storage facilities, LNG terminals and wind turbines. Difficulties and delays in making such investments hamper the ability of the market to respond quickly to demand and thus jeopardise energy security.

Local communities can and should have permitting authority for new facilities. However, since these facilities benefit the country as a whole, the UK government has a role in ensuring that permitting is not unduly delayed. The government is in fact already doing this to a degree and, in a number of cases, quite strongly. It is encouraged to continue and expand upon these activities. A means of facilitating further compensation for the local communities should be explored. In some countries (e.g. Denmark), communities welcome and in fact solicit new wind turbines because they are allowed to invest in the turbines with favourable terms and thus have an interest in seeing new investments go ahead without delay. Providing such added incentives to local communities might encourage areas to accept new infrastructure needed for national energy security.

The UK Energy Review also identifies planning as a major issue to be addressed. It describes the planning barriers facing new energy infrastructure and begins to develop a more effective, better co-ordinated planning process for such projects. While more needs to be done to flesh out and implement these ideas, we commend the government for addressing this issue and we encourage it to move swiftly to resolve it.

Declining oil and gas production will bring increasing dependence on other countries and regions, although this need not represent any real threat to energy security. The experience of the winter of 2005/06 when the UK Interconnector was not used at capacity despite apparent arbitrage opportunities, prompted some UK actors to doubt the reliability of imported energy. In particular, some blamed the continental countries and their less competitive, less transparent gas markets for the UK's supply-demand tightness. The UK is encouraged to continue its work to foster more open liberalised gas markets in other EU countries. However, it may be quite some time before those markets have the type of reform that has been seen in the UK. It would be imprudent to rely too much on this transformation as a necessary step for a secure UK market. The lesson from the winter of 2005/06 regarding imports concerns the value of diversity. Exporting markets can fall short of expectations for a number of technical, political or economic reasons. Castigating those markets for failing to live up to UK standards does little to improve the situation. Ensuring that multiple sources of imports are available from multiple exporting regions – as is now being done by the private sector – is the best way to address uncertainty in any one export area. Thus, the government should promote diversification of energy imports by providing realistic assessments of supply reliability from each region, and by working with the regulator to ensure that the risk to supply reliability is priced in the market.

RECOMMENDATIONS

The government of the United Kingdom should:

▸ *Continue its stated and actual commitment to competitive energy markets as the primary tool for achieving energy policy goals while ensuring a clear and predictable framework for all market participants.*

▸ *Clearly define ways to achieve long-term emissions reduction targets in order to reduce uncertainty and to facilitate investments in supply infrastructure needed to ensure security of supply.*

▸ *Clarify further and provide more details on the investment framework for nuclear power, particularly in the treatment of nuclear waste and decommissioning for new and existing plants.*

‣ *Further improve the availability and quality of data on energy supply, demand and prices to better enable the market to meet security of supply objectives.*

‣ *Seek ways to accelerate planning and licensing procedures for new energy infrastructure.*

‣ *Continue to evaluate the long-term implications of the coming new wave of electricity generating stations in terms of both the effects of long-range carbon reduction objectives and potential over-reliance on certain fuels and technologies (i.e. gas-fired CCGTs).*

‣ *Ensure careful co-ordination between the various departments and authorities with responsibilities for energy and environment-related policy.*

‣ *Continue to take a proactive role in the full implementation of the EU internal energy market while at the same time considering the implications of possible delays in this process for the UK energy policy.*

DOMESTIC GHG EMISSIONS PROFILE AND PROJECTIONS

HISTORICAL EMISSIONS

In 2004, the UK emitted 537 million tonnes of CO_2 (MtCO_2) from fuel combustion.[12] This represented a 3.7% decrease from 1990 and a 0.5% increase from 2003. Natural gas accounted for 37.6% of all emissions from fuel combustion, oil accounted for 35.7% and coal accounted for 26.6%. Since 1990, coal's share of total emissions has fallen substantially, going from 43% of the total to 27% in 2004. In absolute terms, coal-related emissions fell by more than 40% from 1990 to 2004. Oil-related emissions fell by 9% while natural gas emissions rose by more than 90% over the same period.

———————————————— Figure **7**

CO_2 Emissions by Fuel*, 1973 to 2004

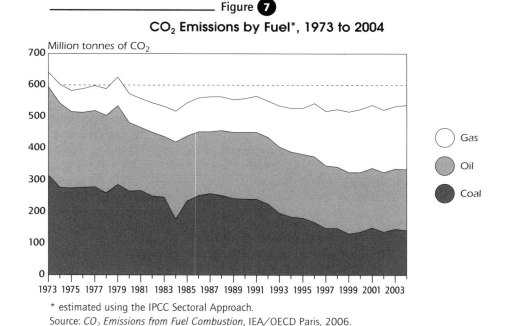

* estimated using the IPCC Sectoral Approach.
Source: *CO_2 Emissions from Fuel Combustion*, IEA/OECD Paris, 2006.

---

12. All figures come from IEA statistics unless otherwise noted.

On a sectoral basis, electricity and heat production accounted for the largest share of CO_2 emissions in 2004, equal to 31% of the total. Transport was the second-most important sector with 24% of the total, followed by residential with 16% and industry with 12%.

——————————— **Figure** **8**

CO_2 Emissions by Sector*, 1973 to 2004

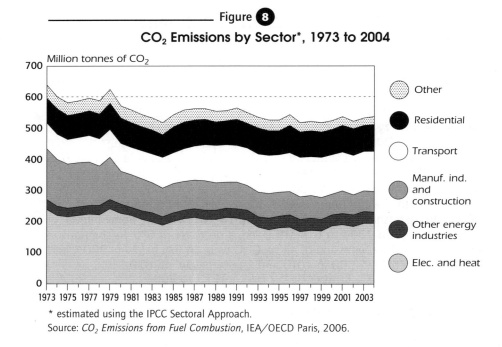

* estimated using the IPCC Sectoral Approach.
Source: *CO_2 Emissions from Fuel Combustion*, IEA/OECD Paris, 2006.

The overall decrease in emissions, the decrease in coal-related emissions and the decrease in emissions from the electricity and heat production all result from the UK's "Dash for Gas". The discovery and production of abundant North Sea natural gas, phase-out of subsidies for domestic coal mining and refinement of technology for combined-cycle gas turbine (CCGT) plants all contributed to a massive change in fuel use – from coal to gas – in the electricity sector. Gas's lower carbon content and the higher efficiency of the CCGT plants resulted in substantial emissions reduction throughout the 1990s.

EMISSION PROJECTIONS

In March 2006, the Department for the Environment, Food and Rural Affairs (Defra) published *Climate Change, The UK Programme 2006*. This document presented forecasts for UK's GHG emissions through 2020. All projections are based on the continuation of existing policies without any additional policies. Basic CO_2 projections are shown in Table 6.

Table **6**

Projection of CO_2 Emissions by Source (Mt of CO_2)

Sector	1990	2004	2010	2015	2020
Energy supply	242.4	212.7	195.8	196.9	180.0
Business	125.8	112.2	110.4	118.4	121.7
Transport	122.8	131.3	135.7	140.4	142.3
Domestic	79.6	89.5	76.3	77.0	77.7
Agriculture	8.1	2.6	–	2.2	4.0
Public	13.6	10.6	11.0	11.4	11.4
Total (less removals by sinks)	**592.2**	**559.2**	**529.1**	**546.3**	**537.5**
% change since 1990		-5.6%	-10.7%	-7.7%	-9.2%

Source: *Climate Change, The UK Programme 2006*, Defra (March 2006).

With regard to the total emissions of all six GHGs, the Climate Programme 2006 forecasts that total emissions from the six will fall from a level of 656 MtCO$_2$-eq[13] in 2004 to 618 MtCO$_2$-eq, a decrease of 6%. In comparison to 1990 levels, total emission of all six GHG were 14.6% below in 2004, and will be 19.4% below 1990 in 2010 and 19.6% below in 2020.

NATIONAL CLIMATE POLICY

EMISSIONS REDUCTION TARGETS

The UK government has a number of different targets for emissions reduction.

- **Kyoto Protocol**. Under the burden-sharing agreement among EU countries, the UK must reduce its GHG emissions by 12.5% below the base year level (1990) for the 2008 to 2012 commitment period.

- **2010 Target**. In 1997, the UK committed itself to go beyond the Kyoto Protocol target by setting a national goal to reduce carbon dioxide emissions by 20% below 1990 levels by 2010.

- **2050 Target**. In 2003, the Energy White Paper adopted a longer-term goal to put the UK on a path to reduce CO_2 emissions by 60% by 2050, with real progress by 2020.

---

13. The UK government usually refers to tonnes of carbon (C) emitted rather than tonnes of carbon dioxide (CO_2) emitted. We have converted all such carbon figures to carbon dioxide to make international comparisons easier. To convert a tonne of C to a tonne of CO_2, multiply by 44/12 (or 3.667).

EMISSIONS REDUCTION OPTIONS

The Climate Change Programme (CCP) of March 2006 includes a range of emissions reduction measures. They are broken down into existing measures and measures still to be implemented.

——————————————————— Table

Existing Measures to Cut Emissions by Sector

Measure	Carbon savings in 2010, $MtCO_2$ compared to 1990 levels
Energy supply	
Renewables Obligation	9.17
Business	
Climate Change Levy	13.57
UK emissions trading scheme (2002-2005)	1.10
Carbon Trust	4.03
Building regulations 2002	1.47
Building regulations 2005	0.73
Climate Change Agreements	10.63
Transport	
Voluntary agreements, including reform of company car taxation and graduated vehicle taxes	8.43
Wider transport measures	2.93
Sustainable distribution (Scotland and Wales)	0.37
Fuel duty escalator	6.97
Domestic	
Energy efficiency commitment (2002-2005)	1.47
Energy efficiency commitment (2006-2008)	2.20
Energy efficiency commitment (2008-2011)	2.20
Building regulations 2002	2.57
Building regulations 2006	2.93
Warm front and fuel poverty programmes	1.47
Market transformation including standards and labelling	0.73
Agriculture	
Woodlands grants scheme	1.83
Woodland planting (Scotland)	1.83
Public sector	–
Central government	0.73
TOTAL	**77.36**

Source: *Climate Change, The UK Programme 2006*, Defra (March 2006).

Table **8**

Measures to be Implemented to Cut Emissions by Sector

Measure	Carbon savings in 2010, $MtCO_2$ compared to 1990 level
Energy supply	
Subsidy for biomass heat	0.37
Second phase of EU Trading Scheme	11.00
Business	
Carbon Trust	0.37
Measures to encourage SMEs to save energy	0.37
Transport	
Renewable transport fuel obligation	5.87
Voluntary agreement with car makers	0.37
Fuel duty escalator	6.97
Domestic	
Increased EEC, 2008-2011	1.83
Energy Performance of Buildings Directive	0.73
Improved efficiency in buildings	0.37
Better billing and metering	0.73
Consumer information and standards	0.73
Agriculture	
Strategy for non-food crops	0.37
Public sector	
Local authorities	0.73
Loans for public sector	0.37
Actions by devolved administrations	0.73
Other measures	0.37
TOTAL	**32.28**

Source: *Climate Change, The UK Programme 2006*, Defra (March 2006).

In April 2006, Defra released a study[14] assessing the cost-effectiveness of the different measures used to cut emissions. The report concludes that the combined net present value of the policies contained in the CCP is positive. Among other results, this report also provides a listing of the cost-effectiveness of policies with the largest GHG emissions savings, shown in Table 9.

---

14. *Synthesis of Climate Change Policy Evaluations,* Department for Environment, Food and Rural Affairs (Defra), April 2006.

—————————————————— Table **9**

Cost-effectiveness of Existing and Planned GHG Emissions Reduction Measures

Policy	Sector	GHG emissions saved (MtCO$_2$-eq)	Cost-effectiveness[1] (GBP/tCO$_2$-eq)
Climate Change Levy	Business	13.55	27.3
Climate Change Agreements	Business	10.63	24.6
Renewables Obligation	Energy supply	9.16	– 47.8
Voluntary agreements	Transport	8.43	– 99.6
Fuel duty escalator	Business, domestic	6.96	68.2
EEC 2002-2011	Domestic	5.86	73.7

1. Indicates the cost of a measure per tonne of CO$_2$ saved. Negative numbers indicate that there is a net benefit of implementing the measure.

Source: *Synthesis of Climate Change Policy Evaluations*, Department for Environment, Food and Rural Affairs (Defra), April 2006.

CRITIQUE

The UK government is a global leader in the fight against climate change with ambitious domestic goals on cutting GHGs and ongoing diplomatic efforts to build consensus on global action. The UK was the first major country to announce a long-term cut in emissions with its 60% reduction target by 2050. It was also instrumental in making energy and climate change a major focus of the 2005 G8 Summit in Gleneagles. In addition, it was one of the first countries to institute a domestic trading scheme for emissions reduction and presented the first, and one of the most stringent, National Allocation Plans (NAPs) to the European Commission for the first phase of the EU-ETS. The government deserves much credit for pushing this issue and this report highly encourages it to continue in the same direction with ongoing implementation of increasingly stronger policies.

In some sense, the UK has been fortunate with its emissions. Thanks to the dash-for-gas, inefficient coal power plants were replaced with more efficient gas-fired power plants and, as a result, even without government efforts, emissions fell substantially. The extent of this reduction is largely played out, however, and the country is unlikely to see additional emissions reductions from this development. Thus, government policies will have to play an increasing role if the country wishes to meet its targets. While emissions reductions from the dash-for-gas were achieved at no real costs for consumers, many future reductions have costs associated with them.

According to the CCP 2006, the UK is currently on track to meet its Kyoto target of reducing GHG emissions by 12.5% in 2008-2012. On the other hand, the more stringent internal target to reduce CO_2 emissions by 20% below 1990 levels by 2010 appears out of reach and will almost certainly not be achieved. Current projections show that based on existing policies, CO_2 emissions in 2010 will be 10.7% below 1990. Even if the most stringent climate policies currently being discussed are implemented in time, the 2010 emissions would still only be 18% below 1990 levels. As for the long-range target of 60% emissions reduction by 2050 with significant progress by 2020, there has been little work done so far on the type of step changes and paradigm shifts that would be needed to achieve such a target. The government is encouraged to investigate ways in which this can be done.

The CCP 2006 provides comprehensive emission projections for all the gases as well as good descriptions of the existing and proposed emissions reduction measures. However, one aspect missing from the document is analysis of the costs that these measures will entail and particularly the cost per tonne of GHG emissions avoided or reduced. Such comparative cost analysis is provided in the Defra study, *Synthesis of Climate Change Policy Evaluations*. These results should be expanded upon and, more importantly, used to determine the proper allocation of resources so as to reduce emissions at the lowest possible cost. Conclusions in the Defra study mirror similar analyses done in other countries, namely that efficiency and demand reduction measures generally offer more cost-effective solutions than supply-side measures.

The high political profile on climate change has led to almost every sector and community in the UK being involved in some kind of climate change programme. The scope of efforts to engage industry and local communities in the objectives of government policy is probably unique among IEA countries and has fostered a high level of awareness of the climate change issue in the UK. This is commendable in that emissions reduction will require the participation of all sectors of the UK economy and society. On the other hand, more cost-effectiveness analysis – as mentioned above – would allow efforts to be concentrated in areas where emissions reductions can be achieved at lowest cost.

The UK wisely uses different measures to tackle emissions in different sectors with each measure designed to be most appropriate for each sector. For example, strict mandatory standards are put in place for the building sector while graduated vehicle taxation based on efficiency is used to curb transport emissions. In other areas, such as emissions trading, more market-based approaches are used. Care must be taken, however, that overlap of multiple policies within any given sector does not unnecessarily complicate or burden that sector. This report sees a risk of such an overlap in two areas. The first is electricity generation. The sector is subject to the Renewables Obligation (RO), the EU-ETS and the Climate Change Levy (CCL). Industry might question a climate change tax on electricity, when the "carbon externality" has been internalised further upstream by generators producing under the EU-ETS cap.

The second sector that can see overlapping measures is the energy-intensive industry covered both by the EU-ETS and the Climate Change Agreements. Under phase I of the EU-ETS, some installations voluntarily opted to be regulated by the EU-ETS, even though they were covered by CCAs. In order to avoid double counting under both schemes, industry and government agreed to net off the EU-ETS surplus from the CCA performance for the first phase of the EU trading scheme. The government is consulting with the relevant sectors through the Emissions Trading Group on arrangements for the second phase. We encourage them to find some type of continuation of the net-off arrangement so that a double benefit from a single emissions reduction or a double penalty from a single emission increase is avoided.

As government and industry learn more about the emissions reduction policy tools on the domestic and international levels, a degree of consolidation should be pursued. This is not to say that the overall effect of this programme should be diminished, but that a more streamlined set of programmes will give more clarity to private actors and minimise the administrative burden for everyone.

RECOMMENDATIONS

The government of the United Kingdom should:

▶ *Develop a clear and streamlined strategy to achieve its objective of reducing carbon emissions by 60% by 2050.*

▶ *Follow through and expand on analysis of the relative cost-effectiveness of the wide variety of measures brought forward in the Climate Change Programme 2006. Concentrate policies in sectors where emissions can be reduced the most and at the lowest cost.*

▶ *Carefully consider the ongoing use of multiple instruments (e.g. CCL, EU-ETS and RO) to reduce emissions from electricity generation.*

▶ *Avoid any overlaps in coverage between the ETS and installations covered by Climate Change Agreements in phase 2 of the ETS.*

ENERGY TRENDS AND INTENSITY MEASURES

Both total primary energy supply (TPES) and total final consumption (TFC) have risen considerably less in the UK than in the OECD countries as a whole. The UK TPES in 2004 was 234 Mtoe, only 6% higher than in 1973. The OECD countries as a whole saw an increase in TPES of 46% over the same period.[15] The modest UK TPES growth is largely a result of decreased coal use and its replacement by more efficient energy sources. In 2004, the UK TFC was 164 Mtoe, an increase of 11% since 1973. TFC grew by 35% for the OECD countries as a whole over the same period. These trends have continued in recent years. From 2000 to 2004, UK TPES grew by a total of 0.3% (compared to 3.4% for the OECD as a whole) and TFC grew by 1.6% (compared to 4.0% for the OECD).

In 2004, UK aggregate energy intensity, as measured by a ratio of the country's TPES in tonnes of oil equivalent (toe) over its national gross domestic product (GDP, in thousands of 2000 USD), was 0.147 toe per USD 1 000. This was the fifth-lowest energy intensity in the IEA (behind Japan, Switzerland, Denmark and Ireland) and 26% below the OECD average. Figure 8 compares UK national energy intensity to the IEA average as well as to selected countries.

Such snapshot aggregate measures of energy intensity, however, can lack statistical integrity. For example, the results depend to a great extent on the choice of a base year for the GDP figures and the means chosen to get national GDPs portrayed in the same units for all countries (whether by exchange rates or purchasing power parity. In addition, the numbers are heavily influenced by economic structure (*e.g.* the presence of energy-intensive industry) and geography (*e.g.* cold winters and hot summers). An alternative and often more revealing analysis can be gained from observing the progression of the intensity figures over time. From 1973 to 2004, UK TPES per unit of GDP fell by 46%. Over the same period, this intensity ratio fell by 36% for the OECD as a whole. Shorter-term measures also show UK's reductions to be more pronounced than the OECD as a whole. Table 10 looks at the fall in energy intensity over a range of time periods for the UK, the IEA as a whole and five other IEA countries.

Disaggregated measures of efficiency and/or intensity can help identify areas in an economy where a country may be more or less energy-efficient compared to other countries. At the same time, such measures can be misleading

---

15. This and all averages in this section represent a weighted average of countries' data.

Figure **9**

Energy Intensity in the UK and in Other Selected IEA Countries, 1973 to 2010

(toe per thousand USD at 2000 prices and purchasing power parities)

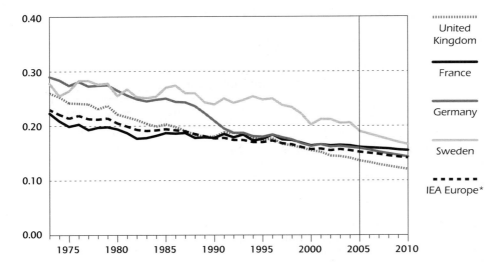

* excluding Luxembourg and Norway throughout the series, as forecast data are not available for these countries.

Sources: *Energy Balances of OECD Countries*, IEA/OECD Paris, 2006; *National Accounts of OECD Countries*, OECD Paris, 2006 and country submissions.

Table **10**

Decrease in Energy Intensity Measured as TPES/GDP

(toe per thousand 2000 USD)

Country	1973 to 2004	1983 to 2004	1993 to 2004
United Kingdom	–46%	–31%	–24%
France	–26%	–8%	–11%
Germany	–44%	–34%	–14%
Australia	–24%	–21%	–17%
United States	–46%	–31%	–20%
Japan	–26%	–4%	+1%
IEA total[1]	–36%	–21%	–12%

1. Weighted average of all countries.

Source: *Energy Balances of OECD Countries*, IEA/OECD Paris, 2005.

because the relevant country characteristics can vary so much. Important differences could be the size and type of a country's industry, climate and geographic size, and distances to be travelled. A series of data from IEA analyses is provided in Table 12 which compares UK energy use to other

—————————————————— Table ⑪

Measurements of Energy Use by Sector for the UK and Other IEA Countries

	UK	US	France	Germany	Japan
Energy use per unit of manufacturing added value, MJ/USD (1999)	6.99	~ 9.40	7.10	6.37	7.30
Energy use per unit of service sector added value, MJ/USD	1.10	1.36	1.11	1.07	0.85
Car fleet average fuel intensity, l/100 km	8.96	10.89	7.41	8.49	7.69
Residential energy use, GJ/capita (1998)[1]	31.48	41.25	34.05	30.05	19.28

1. Residential energy use is normalised for climate based on degree days. It includes space heating, water heating, cooking, lighting and appliances.

Source: *30 Years of Energy Use in IEA Countries*, IEA (2004).

—————————————————— Table ⑫

Measurements of Energy Intensity by Sector for the UK and Other IEA Countries

(figures show final consumption in each sector per national GDP, toe per thousand 2000 USD)

	UK	France	Australia	Average[1]
Industry	0.025	0.027	0.040	0.039
Residential	0.027	0.031	0.016	0.025
Commerce and public services	0.010	0.009	0.010	0.015
Transport	0.033	0.032	0.050	0.044

1. Weighted average of all the OECD countries.

Source: *Energy Balances of OECD Countries*, IEA/OECD Paris, 2006.

countries by sector. Such data can be very instructive but, because of the many extraneous factors, should be considered indicative rather than providing a direct measure of each country's efficiency in each sector.

GENERAL GOVERNMENT EFFICIENCY POLICY

In recent years, energy efficiency has emerged as one of the government's primary tools in meeting its energy policy objectives. The Energy White Paper of 2003 made a strong case for improved efficiency, stating that "the cheapest, cleanest and safest way of addressing our energy policy objectives is to use less energy". The White Paper elaborated a vision whereby half the expected emissions reductions through 2020 would come from improved efficiency. Subsequent annual reports on the implementation of the Energy White Paper track the progress made in this area.

In April 2004, the government released *Energy Efficiency: the Government's Plan for Action*. This report further examines the potential savings identified in the White Paper and lays out plans to save over 44 million tonnes (Mt) of additional CO_2 through energy efficiency by 2010. It divides energy consumers into households and business and public sector with 15.4 $MtCO_2$ savings coming from households and 28.95 $MtCO_2$ from business and the public sector. The Plan does not cover transport.

In December 2005, the government published the Energy *Efficiency Innovation Review: Summary Report*. This report summarises the conclusions of the Energy Efficiency Innovation Review (EEIR) launched jointly by Defra and HM Treasury in the Pre-Budget Report 2004. The document offers a detailed analysis of the scope, costs and benefits of enhanced action on energy efficiency. It states that while the UK has made good progress in reducing emissions, substantial new action would be needed to meet the goal of reducing CO_2 emissions by 20% below 1990 levels by 2010. The report analyses existing programmes in the household and business sectors and various ways to effectively expand them. It also considers new demand-side efficiency technologies.

The Climate Change Programme (CCP), published on 28 March 2006, provides further details on government plans for improving efficiency. This programme lays out the full range of existing and proposed measures to curb carbon emissions. Efficiency and other demand-side efforts feature prominently in all sectors.

Defra provides the following data on the potential for emissions reduction for a range of energy efficiency measures:

_____ Table **13**
Carbon Savings through Energy Efficiency

	Savngs per year by 2010 (MtCO$_2$)
Households	
Building regulations	5.5
Energy Efficiency Commitment	6.9 - 8
Warm Front	1.5
Other measures	2.6
Sub-total	17.6
Business and public sector	
Climate Change Agreements	10.6
The Carbon Trust	4.0
Building regulations (non housing)	2.2
Public sector	1.1
Other	1.8
Sub-total	19.8
Overall total	**66.7**

Source: Defra Web site.

HOUSEHOLD SECTOR ENERGY POLICIES

THE ENERGY EFFICIENCY COMMITMENT (EEC)

The EEC is the principal policy mechanism driving improved efficiency in existing homes. Under the EEC, electricity and gas suppliers are required to achieve targets for energy efficiency improvements in the household sector. These targets do not prescribe the exact manner in which suppliers should attain these improvements. Instead, suppliers can fulfil their obligations by carrying out any combination of approved measures including installing insulation or supplying and promoting low-energy light bulbs, high-efficiency appliances or boilers. Suppliers must achieve all their savings in the household sector and at least half of their savings obligation must come from households which receive income-related benefits and/or tax credits, the so-called "priority sector".

The suppliers are not accorded any explicit supplemental revenue to compensate them for the costs of achieving their savings obligations. Since they are in a competitive market with other firms threatening to capture their market share, they can pass through as much percentage of these added costs as possible. Many suppliers are using their EEC obligations as an opportunity to get close to their customers and enhance brand awareness.

Expanding Levels of Savings in the EEC Phases

The first phase of the EEC ran from April 2002 to March 2005. Energy suppliers successfully met their targets and were able to bank additional activity into the next phase of the scheme. EEC 2002-2005 is expected to save 1.36 $MtCO_2$ annually by 2010. The current phase of EEC running from April 2005 to March 2008 will deliver roughly twice the level of activity of EEC 2002-2005 and is expected to achieve carbon savings of around 2.27 $MtCO_2$ annually by 2010. The CCP of March 2006 recently announced the intention to expand the EEC further, targeting around 4.0 of annual $MtCO_2$ savings for EEC3, the period 2008-2011. Table 14 shows the continuing growth of this programme in its different phases.

Table 14

Progression of Scope for the EEC Programme

	EEC1 2002-2005	EEC2 2005-2008	EEC3 2008-2011	Accumulated total 2000-2011
Annual carbon savings, $MtCO_2$	1.5	2.2	4.0	7.7
% of emissions from residential sector	1.0%	1.5%	2.7%	5.2%
% of total UK emissions[1]	0.3%	0.4%	0.7%	1.4%
Total energy savings, TWh[2]	62	130	204[1]	396

1. Approximation.

2. The values in this row are derived from the formulae the government uses to determine savings for each measure implemented. Since it involves discounting the savings from future years, the actual level of savings over the lifetime of the projects will be greater.

Sources: Ofgem; British Gas; *CO₂ Emissions from Fuel Combustion*, IEA/OECD Paris, 2005.

EEC Administration

While EEC policy and targets are shaped by Defra, programme operation is handled by the regulator, Ofgem. This includes setting suppliers' targets, assessing proposals for savings schemes, monitoring activity, approving compliance schemes and enforcing compliance when necessary. The savings realised by suppliers for any specific measure implemented are calculated in the following way. First, a determination is made for both business-as-usual energy use and energy use with the measure put in place. The annual energy savings is the difference between the two. This annual energy saving is then discounted over the expected lifetime of the measure. Finally, the discounted energy saving is fuel-standardised. This takes into account the carbon content of the fuel being displaced and thus determines each measure's level of emissions reduction.

The table below shows the measures allowable under the EEC scheme:

Table

Energy Efficiency Measures Accredited under EEC1
(measures in bold accounted for 98.7% of savings realised)

Cavity wall insulation	Jug kettles
Loft insulation	**Condensing boilers**
DIY loft insulation	**Heating controls**
Draught stripping	**Thermostatic radiator valves**
Hot water tank insulation	**New central heating**
External wall cladding	**Upgraded heating**
Insulation of pipes and valves	Ground sourced heat pumps
Radiator panels	Combined heat and power
Refrigerators	Upgrading district heating boiler
Fridge-freezers	Kiltox heat fans
Freezers	**Compact fluorescent lamps (CFLs)**
Washing machines	**Luminaires designed solely for CFLs**
Dishwashers	

Source: *Evaluation of the Energy Efficiency Commitment 2002-05*, Eoin Lees Energy, 28 February 2006.

A target was set for twelve supplier groups under EEC1: Atlantic Electric and Gas, British Gas, Cambridge Gas, Dee Valley, EDF Energy, RWE npower, Opus Energy, Powergen, Scottish and Southern Energy, Scottish Power, Telecom Plus and TXY Energi. Obligated suppliers that do not meet their targets are subjected to penalties equal to 10% of their revenue. Thus far, no supplier has failed to meet the targets except for TXU Energi which went into administration in 2002 and Atlantic Electric and Gas which went into administrative receivership in 2004. While savings obligations can technically be traded among suppliers, very little of this activity has taken place.

Results

The results of the EEC have so far been positive. Suppliers have met – and very often exceeded – their targets, and the costs for doing so have been less than expected by Defra. During the three-year period of EEC1 (2002-2005), measures put in place are expected to result in 86.8 TWh of savings. This is nearly 40% higher than the target of 227 MtCO$_2$ of savings from that time period. The "extra" savings can be carried over to the EEC2 (2005-2008). Savings in the priority sector were around 45 TWh, while those in the non-priority sectors were around 42 TWh. The figure below shows how much each set of measures contributed to the total savings for all obligated suppliers.

Energy Savings by Measure Type as a Percentage of Total Savings for EEC1

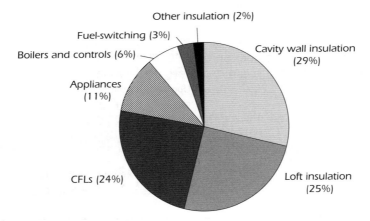

Source: *Energy Efficiency Commitment Update,* Issue 13, August 2005; Ofgem.

Results thus far for EEC2 (2005-2008) show that savings are being achieved at rates well above the obligation levels. The carry-overs from EEC1 equal 27% of the suppliers' EEC2 obligations for the whole three-year period. EEC2 activity from April 2005 through year-end 2005 generated another 21% of the savings obligation. In addition, anecdotal evidence suggests that, in part because of the high UK energy prices seen this past winter, a great deal of energy savings activity has taken place thus far in 2006. Thus, it is likely that suppliers will meet their EEC2 obligations without undue difficulty and are likely to again carry-over substantial savings to the subsequent period.

In its February 2006 report to Defra on the EEC1,[16] Eoin Lees Energy calculates that the EEC1 measures have been realised at a total cost of 1.3 pence (p) per kWh for electricity and 0.5p per kWh for gas. These figures include all costs from both the obligated supplier and the consumer who may contribute to some of the cost of the measures implemented. The cost of savings for both electricity and gas are less than the consumer prices for these fuels, which the report cites as 6.7p per kWh for electricity and 1.7p per kWh for gas in 2004. (These consumer prices have risen significantly in 2005 and 2006.)

As for the effect on customers' bills, Eoin Lees Energy in the same report calculates that the average customer's bill has risen by GBP 3.18 per year per fuel. This is around 20% less than the expected customer bill increase estimated by Defra. Ofgem estimated in April 2006 that for EEC2, the likely increase to each customer's bill will be GBP 9 per fuel per year. To put this indicative figure in context, energy bills in the UK currently average GBP 330 and GBP 520 per year for electricity and gas respectively.[17] Of course, the activity of the suppliers and the degree to which they must financially encourage consumers to implement energy-saving measures is inversely related to energy prices. High energy prices – and public and press attention to these prices – will motivate consumers to be more energy-efficient even if there were no supplier activities on the EEC. It is therefore possible that the amount suppliers need to spend to achieve their savings obligations will be less than anticipated for EEC2.

Defra has estimated[18] that the measures implemented in EEC1 resulted in a negative cost of around GBP 82 per tonne of CO_2 emissions reduced. In other words, the measures were cost-effective without taking the benefits of reduced emissions into account.

DECENT HOMES

In July 2000 the government established the target that all social housing should meet established standards of decency by 2010. Since 2001 there has been a 20% reduction in the number of social sector homes failing the standard on the thermal comfort criterion. Also since 2001, over 470 000 dwellings have received work to improve their energy efficiency under the Decent Homes programme or as part of wider local authority work to update the stock. This work is ongoing and is accelerating towards the 2010 target.

---

16. *Evaluation of the Energy Efficiency Commitment 2002-05*, Eoin Lees Energy, 28 February 2006.
17. Energywatch, February 2006.
18. "Assessment of EEC 2002-05 Carbon, Energy and Cost Savings", Defra, April 2006.

The average Standard Assessment Procedure rating of the social sector stock rose from 48 in 1996 to 57 by 2003 and is likely to rise further over the coming years. The Decent Homes standard is a "trigger point" for action to improve energy efficiency. As social landlords undertake works beyond the standard, energy efficiency improvements are accelerating, which in turn reduces carbon emissions.

BUILDING REGULATIONS

Building regulations are steadily driving up the energy standards of new and refurbished buildings. For example, a house built to the 2002 standards uses about half the energy consumed in the average existing house. The 2002 building regulations are expected to deliver reductions in carbon dioxide emissions in 2010 of 2.55 $MtCO_2$ in the household sector. The same building regulations do not apply UK-wide: those in England and Wales are shared, while Northern Ireland and Scotland have separate regulations.

In September 2005, the government announced further changes to the building regulations to make buildings more energy-efficient. From April 2006, these new measures have delivered increased energy standards for new buildings of around 27% in non-domestic buildings, 22% in houses and 18% in flats. On average, the energy efficiency improvement in dwellings will be 20%, which reflects in part the growing proportion of flats being built for people living alone.

The new measures, together with the 2002 revisions, will improve new build standards by 40% and could cut fuel bills by an equivalent amount for new homes built from 2006 compared to pre-April 2002 new build. The latest changes to new building standards and requirements for condensing boilers are expected to deliver carbon savings of around 2.75 $MtCO_2$ per year by 2010. One provision of the revised building regulations came into force in April 2005, requiring all new and replacement boilers to be at least B-rated, subject to some exemptions. This has had the effect of rapidly increasing the market share of the most efficient condensing boilers. Condensing boilers are expected to deliver carbon savings of around 3.3 $MtCO_2$ in 2010.

The government recently published its Code for Sustainable Homes. This system will rate new homes to give buyers a clear, easy to understand measure of each house's environmental footprint. In addition to measuring each house's level of energy efficiency, the Code will also establish standards for water use, waste management and use of materials. The Code will be performance-based and, as such, does not specify how the Code's standards are achieved, which is left to the builder. Minimum performance levels will be set for each criterion and in cases where a relevant building code already exists, this minimum must at least equal or exceed it. The Code currently has five levels. The lowest level simply assures that the house meets the threshold levels for all the criteria. Three higher levels will be for houses that exceed the minimum requirements to varying degrees. The fifth level will be for houses which deliver 80% or more of the Code's optimal standards. All government-funded houses must at least achieve Code level 3.

SUSTAINABLE COMMUNITIES/COMMUNITY ENERGY

Community Energy is a GBP 50m UK-wide capital grant programme funded from the Treasury's Capital Modernisation Fund to increase the development and installation of community heating schemes. The first bidding round under the programme was held in January 2002. Its aim was to address the key barriers of a lack of investment capital and a lack of knowledge on how to deliver the benefits of community heating. The programme intends to deliver carbon savings and help alleviate fuel poverty through lower energy bills. Schemes mainly based on CHP with innovative approaches, such as energy from waste, are also encouraged.

An additional GBP 10 million was announced in December 2004 to extend the programme to 31 March 2008. This decision was based on strong demand for funding in early bidding rounds, including a number of larger schemes with significant outputs. However, experience has shown that, largely because of the limited time span of the programme with a spend deadline of 31 March 2007, many of these larger schemes did not go ahead. By contrast, the smaller schemes that can be completed within the programme's time frame tend to be expensive in relation to the outputs they deliver. The following table summarises how the programme has delivered against the targets originally set for it.

——————————————— Table

Comparison of Outputs against Targets for Phase I of the Community Energy Programme

	Programme targets	Estimate of total outputs from programme
Funding	GBP 50 m	GBP 22.3 m (45%)
Carbon savings (tCO$_2$/yr)	550 000	71 378 (13%)
Leverage of other funding	GBP 200 m	GBP 50 m (25%)
CHP capacity (MWe)	130	28.9 (22%)
People on low incomes helped	100 000	18 453 (18%)

Source: Energy Saving Trust.

The high drop-out rate for larger schemes is reflected in the limited estimate of expenditure. This is despite the government's expectation of some drop-out of schemes by over-allocating funds against the budget of GBP 50 million.

FUEL POVERTY

Addressing and reducing fuel poverty is one of the four major objectives of UK energy policy. A household is in fuel poverty if, in order to maintain a satisfactory heating regime, it would be required to spend more than 10% of its income (including housing benefit or income support for mortgage interest) on household fuel use. Fuel poverty is caused by a combination of poorly insulated, energy-inefficient housing and low incomes. The latest available figures[19] indicate that the number of fuel-poor households remained broadly unchanged between 2003 and 2004. There were approximately 2 million households in fuel poverty in the UK in 2004, down from 6.5 million in 1996. Of this figure, around 1.5 million vulnerable households (i.e. households with children, or someone who is elderly, sick or disabled) were in fuel poverty in the UK in 2003, down from 5 million in 1996. Recent increases in fuel costs will have worsened fuel poverty since 2004.

In Fuel Poverty In England: The Government's Plan for Action, published in November 2004, the government set out how the 2010 target in England[20] will be met and announced extra funding of GBP 140 million between 2005 and 2008 to tackle fuel poverty. This has since been boosted by the announcement in the 2005 Pre-Budget Report of an additional GBP 300 m over the same period to tackle fuel poverty across the UK. GBP 250 m of this funding will help tackle fuel poverty in England, taking total fuel poverty funding over the 2005-2008 period to over GBP 800 m CO_2 savings from the Warm Front, and other fuel poverty programmes are expected to be 1.5 $MtCO_2$ by 2010.

The document also sets out a number of changes to the Warm Front scheme, the government's key tool for tackling fuel poverty in the private sector in England, which seeks to target vulnerable households to provide a range of heating and insulation measures that can be tailored to suit each individual property. These changes have been implemented. Warm Front now offers central heating to all eligible households and gives them the option to receive the full range of appropriate measures over a period of time, subject to the maximum amount of grant that can be paid. Since the launch of the scheme in June 2000, over one million households have been assisted.

---

19. *The UK Fuel Poverty Strategy: Fourth Annual Progress Report*, published in June 2006.
20. "To eradicate fuel poverty in vulnerable households in line with the Gouvernment's fuel poverty strategic objective".

METERING AND BILLING

The government believes that providing energy consumption feedback to consumers is another key measure to encourage energy efficiency at home. The Energy End-Use Efficiency and Energy Services Directive will require installation of time-of-use metering for all new connections and for replacement meters where "technically possible, financially reasonable and proportionate to the potential savings". The government estimates that about 0.73 MtCO$_2$ per year could be saved by 2010 with better billing and metering if from 2008 all new and replacement meters are "smart" meters, also providing consumption feedback. The savings would increase over time as more meters are installed. However, there is great uncertainty about the scale and duration of these carbon savings.

The government believes that smart meters have not only the potential to reduce consumption but also to diminish peak loads, for example via time-of-day tariffs. Smart meters can therefore contribute to improving energy security, as some network reinforcement and new generating capacity could be avoided. However, smart meters are expensive and so the government announced the launch of a series of trials to determine the cost-effectiveness of smart meters before determining its final policy. These trials were scheduled to start at the end of 2006 with results available from mid-2007 onwards.

As part of the Energy Review, the government carried out an analysis of the impact of improvements to domestic billing and concluded that the provision of historic information in the form of graphs comparing previous with present energy consumption was a useful and very cost-effective way to stimulate consumers to save energy. It will, therefore, be mandating changes to customers' bills from 2007 onwards.

Despite their potential benefits, very few smart meters have been installed in the UK. Ofgem's review of metering looked at international experience of smart metering and, in the light of this evidence, is examining the potential costs and benefits of innovative metering in the UK context. Ofgem conducted a public consultation which closed in mid-March 2006. Ofgem concluded that smart meters could indeed bring benefits to both energy suppliers and their customers and that a competitive market was the best way to deliver them. They also concluded that regulatory barriers and lack of inter-operability hindered their widespread use in the UK. Ofgem is therefore working with industry to develop common standards and to remove barriers to their introduction

The Energy Review also looked at the role of portable display devices which can be used to show electricity users real-time information on their energy consumption. These devices are much cheaper than smart meters and international evidence indicates that they can help households make substantial savings on their energy bills. The government is considering the best way to stimulate the introduction of such devices to UK households.

MARKET TRANSFORMATION PROGRAMME

The government's Market Transformation Programme (MTP) aims to drive and underpin sustainable improvements in the energy efficiency of products. MTP uses policy tools to assess and rank the performance of energy-using products; to establish performance information, including labels; to encourage innovation and competition; and to identify appropriate levels for minimum, average, or best practice standards.

The eco-design of the Energy-Using Products (EUPs) framework directive now provides a powerful formal mechanism for establishing product standards. EUP permits EU member states and the European Commission itself to signal to industry its product innovation priorities, to negotiate and, if necessary, to set mandatory energy and other eco-design requirements for energy-using products which are placed on the EU market. The Commission estimates that this measure alone could reduce EU energy consumption by around 10%, while a recent IEA study on energy savings in California attributes 30% of all energy saved to product standards of the type envisaged in EUPs. The UK government has already committed to proactively follow this policy approach and, supported by the Market Transformation Programme, is actively determining UK priorities to negotiate with the Commission and other member States. The Commission has identified 14 priority product sectors, including consumer electronics, lighting, heating, white goods and electric motors.

The UK is also engaging with its major electronics retailers to establish a Retailer Initiative. The initiative, announced by HM Treasury, will develop a voluntary agreement to promote the sale of more energy-efficient consumer electronics. Discussions are at a very early stage.

ENERGY SAVING TRUST

The Energy Saving Trust (EST) is an independent body funded by the government to promote energy savings and emissions reductions in the household sector. EST's activities are designed to underpin and complement the work of other actors in energy efficiency markets. In particular it seeks to work with the key government policy drivers for household energy efficiency – EEC, Warm Front, Decent Homes and building regulations. Its principal activities are aimed at increasing demand for energy efficiency by raising awareness, providing advice and support for action. It also supports the supply of energy efficiency products and services to meet this demand by developing partnerships, stimulating innovation, supporting training and providing accreditation.

EST's energy efficiency activity is grant-funded by Defra. The Trust also receives funding from Scottish Executive, from the Department of Transport to run transport programmes and from the Department of Trade and Industry to run renewable energy programmes.

BUSINESS SECTOR ENERGY POLICIES

CLIMATE CHANGE LEVY

The government introduced the Climate Change Levy (CCL) in April 2001. The CCL is a tax on energy products paid by the majority of the manufacturing and services sectors of industry, as well as public bodies. Rates for the CCL were based on carbon content of fuels at the time of introduction, based on UK averages, and they were set at:

- 0.15p per kWh for gas.

- 1.17p per kg (equivalent to 0.15p per kWh) for coal.

- 0.96p per kg (equivalent to 0.07p per kWh) for liquefied petroleum gas (LPG).

- 0.43p per kWh for electricity.

The 2006 Pre-Budget announced that the CCL would be increased with inflation as of 1 April 2007.

CCL does not apply to fuels used by the domestic or transport sectors, or fuels used for the production of other forms of energy (such as for electricity generation) or for non-energy purposes. It does not apply to oil, which is already subject to excise duty. Energy used by small firms is also excluded. There are also several additional exemptions from the levy, including:

- Electricity generated from [new] renewables.

- Fuel used by Good Quality CHP.

- Fuels used as feedstock.

- Electricity used for electrolysis processes, such as the chlo-alkali process or primary aluminium smelting.

The horticulture sector, which is relatively energy-intensive, contains a large number of smaller companies and is exposed to significant international competition, was given a temporary 50% discount on the levy for a five-year period. This sector has now qualified for a full climate change agreement under the new eligibility criteria (see section below) and growers who previously enjoyed the discount are eligible to join this new agreement.

The CCL is structured to encourage businesses to improve their energy efficiency levels. Improving energy efficiency can help to deliver a double dividend of both reduced emissions and enhanced business competitiveness. To ensure that the levy was introduced in a way that supported business competitiveness, it was accompanied by a 0.3% cut in employers' National Insurance contributions, worth approximately GBP 1.2 billion in 2004/05, compared with the GBP 772 million raised by the levy in the same year.

Enhanced capital allowances (ECAs) were also introduced to encourage the use of energy-saving technologies. ECAs are now available for 15 different categories of technology and 13 000 different products. In addition, the Carbon Trust was established to give support and advice to business. Combined with the incentive to improve energy efficiency levels provided by the CCL, these other measures have allowed businesses to make the necessary adaptations.

An independent evaluation by Cambridge Econometrics has examined the effect of the levy since its announcement in the 1999 Budget and introduction in April 2001. This study found that the CCL could deliver annual carbon savings of over 3.5 MtC in 2010 – substantially above the 2 MtC estimated at the time of its introduction. According to this evaluation, the impact was largely due to an announcement effect, with a smaller reduction in demand due to the price effect from the levy feeding through into higher fuel prices. The impact of the levy in the DTI projections is part of the EUP baseline.

CLIMATE CHANGE AGREEMENTS

Recognising the need to maintain the competitiveness of energy-intensive sectors subject to international competition, CCAs were introduced alongside the CCL. CCAs provide an 80% discount from the levy for those sectors that agree to meet targets to improve energy efficiency or reduce GHG emissions. The climate change agreements are negotiated between relevant trade associations and Defra. The agreements operate on two levels with targets for both sectors and individual operators. Sector-level umbrella agreements detail the facilities covered by the agreement and the relevant process. They also list sector targets, and the conditions which apply to participating companies. Participants in the agreements determine how best to lower energy use. They can meet their targets by trading emission allowances either with other companies in an agreement or with companies taking part in the voluntary UK emissions trading scheme.

Eligibility to enter CCAs was initially dependent on criteria based on the Pollution and Prevention Control Regulations 2000, which implement the EU Directive (EC/96/61) on integrated pollution prevention and control. Forty-two sectors with around 10 000 facilities are covered by agreements under these eligibility criteria. Budget 2004 announced that the eligibility criteria would be extended to cover other energy-intensive sectors if they exceed energy intensity thresholds and, in some cases, a test of international competition. A further ten sectors with over 300 facilities have completed negotiations and five of these have been granted state aid approval by the European Commission. The remainder are expected to obtain approval in the near future.

In order to continue to receive the discount on the CCL, facilities must achieve the energy efficiency (or emissions reduction) targets set out in the agreements. Performance is tested every two years up to 2010. At the second target period in 2004, sectors again performed well against their targets, with a total of the absolute savings from each sector compared to its base year of 14.3 $MtCO_2$ per annum. Although in the first target period in 2002, a large proportion of the savings were a result of reduced output in the steel sector. In 2004, output had risen by 28% over the 2002 level, and is forecast to rise further up to 2010. Nevertheless, energy use in the steel sector rose by only 10%, indicating that the steel sector is continuing to improve its energy efficiency.

Targets for 2006 to 2010 were reviewed during 2004 and 2005 to ensure that they continued to represent the potential for cost-effective energy savings while taking into account any changes in technical and market circumstances. The Energy Review took account of the better-than-expected performance for the majority of sectors in the first target period. For the largest sectors that are also affected by the EU Emissions Trading Scheme (EU-ETS), the revised targets were taken into account in setting the allocations under the UK National Allocation Plan (NAP).

The target reviews have, overall, resulted in forecasting additional savings by 2010 (over business as usual) of 1 $MtCO_2$ above the 9.2 $MtCO_2$ predicted in 2001. The additional savings from sectors excluding steel is 1.7 $MtCO_2$. The forecast increase in production from the steel sector up to 2010, which is reflected in the targets, allows a net increase in emissions of 0.73 $MtCO_2$ for this sector. It is estimated that the climate change agreements will, in aggregate, save 10.5 $MtCO_2$ per annum by 2010. These savings are included in the baseline with measures projection.

Around 500 installations in the first phase of the EU Emissions Trading Scheme are also at least partially covered by CCAs. The UK has obtained temporary exclusion for 331 of these, with the remainder opting to go into the scheme. To apply equivalent reporting arrangements with the EU-ETS, which is a requirement of the directive, the target units containing a temporarily excluded installation will report their CCA performance annually for the duration of the exclusion.

For those installations opting to enter the EU-ETS, there may be overlaps in coverage with the CCAs. For example, if a company lowers energy use as part of the CCA (and is rewarded through a reduced CCL), it would at the same time lower its emissions and be able to sell more allowances in the EU-ETS. Therefore, this company would benefit under two different schemes for the same action. Alternatively, if energy use and emissions rose, installations would face the negative consequences of both systems. Industry preferred a mechanism to net off the EU-ETS surplus from the CCA performance to the alternative of taking out the EU-ETS emissions from the CCA target. This procedure is in place for the first phase of the EU Trading Scheme, but the government is consulting with the sectors through the Emissions Trading Group on arrangements for the second phase.

CARBON TRUST

The Carbon Trust is an independent company funded by the government. It was established in April 2001, at the same time as the Climate Change Levy was introduced, to facilitate the UK move towards a low-carbon economy by helping business and the public sector save energy and reduce carbon dioxide emissions, and by capturing the commercial opportunities of low-carbon technologies. It provides independent information and impartial advice on energy saving and carbon management through site visits, events and case studies.

Carbon management is a systematic approach to support core business strategy looking at every aspect of an organisation's performance in relation to climate change. The Carbon Management Programme has worked with more than 200 large companies, 63 local authorities and five major government departments.

The Carbon Trust also promotes the Enhanced Capital Allowances Scheme to encourage investment by business in qualifying energy-saving technologies and products, and manages the list of qualifying equipment. Companies can claim 100% first-year allowances against investment in qualifying technologies.

The Carbon Trust launched a pilot Energy Efficiency Loan Scheme for small and medium-sized enterprises (SMEs) in 2002. It provides interest-free loans of between GBP 5 000 and GBP 100 000 for up to four years for qualifying energy efficiency projects. The purpose of the scheme is to overcome a common barrier to investment where the project is financially viable but the capital budget is constrained by short-term cash flow requirements. The Scottish Executive funds an equivalent scheme in Scotland called Loan Action Scotland.

EMISSIONS TRADING SCHEME

In April 2002, the government established the first economy-wide GHG emissions trading scheme (UK-ETS). This voluntary pilot scheme, which ends in 2006, has 33 participants who receive government incentive money in return for meeting emissions reduction targets. The scheme was set up to enable "learning by doing" for both participants and government ahead of international emissions trading. UK firms also participate in the European Union Emissions Trading Scheme (EU-ETS). The current operation of this scheme is described in detail in the Energy and Climate Change chapter. The financial incentive to reduce emissions under the schemes leads firms in the programme to reduce their energy use.

COMBINED HEAT AND POWER (CHP)

CHP is an important element in the government's energy policy. In 2000, the government set a new target to achieve at least 10 000 MWe of installed Good Quality CHP capacity by 2010. In addition, the government has also recently set a target to source at least 15% of electricity for use on the Government Estate from Good Quality CHP by 2010.

In April 2004, Defra published the *Government's Strategy for Combined Heat and Power to 2010*. The strategy incorporates the full range of measures to support the growth of CHP capacity needed to meet the CHP target, and lay the foundation for long-term growth in CHP. Since 2000, the government has introduced a package of measures to support CHP, including those in the strategy. These measures are categorised below.

Fiscal Incentives

- Exemption from the Climate Change Levy for all Good Quality CHP fuel inputs and electricity outputs.

- Climate Change Agreements to provide an incentive for emissions reductions.

- Eligibility for Enhanced Capital Allowances (ECAs) to stimulate investment.

- Business Rates exception for CHP power generation plant and machinery.

- A reduction in VAT on certain domestic micro-CHP installations.

- The GBP 50 million Community Energy Programme to encourage CHP in community heating schemes, which ran through to 31 March 2005.

Grant Support

- The Community Energy Programme to encourage CHP in community heating schemes.

- Bioenergy Capital Grants scheme (now closed to applicants).

Regulatory Framework

- The UK and EU Emissions Trading Schemes.

- Introduction of the EU Cogeneration Directive.

- Changes to the licensing regime, benefiting smaller generators.

- Working with Ofgem, to ensure a level playing field under the New Electricity Trading Arrangements (NETA) for smaller generators, including CHP.

- Emphasising CHP benefits when planning or when sustainable development guidance is reviewed or introduced.

- Review of procedures on power station consents applications to ensure full consideration of CHP.

- Exploring opportunities to give incentives for CHP under any future Energy Efficiency Commitment (EEC).

- Encouraging the uptake of CHP through the building regulations.

- Research and development into CHP by the Carbon Trust.

Promotion of Innovation

- Promotion and support by the Carbon Trust and Energy Savings Trust for the development of energy efficiency and low-carbon technologies, and ensure their programmes reinforce delivery of the 10 000 MWe target.

- Instigation of field trials to evaluate the benefits of micro-CHP.

- Improvements to existing CHP schemes through the development of a Quality Improvement programme.

Government Leadership and Partnership

- Adoption of a 15% target for government departments to use CHP-generated electricity.

- Encouragement of other parts of the public sector to consider setting similar targets.

TRANSPORT AND ENERGY EFFICIENCY

The government has in place a number of policies to promote the uptake of fuel-efficient vehicles. The policy framework for supporting cleaner vehicles was laid out in the July 2002 report from the Department of Transport, *Powering Future Vehicles Strategy*. This ten-year strategy has two primary goals:

- To promote the development, introduction and uptake of clean, low-carbon vehicles and fuels.

- To ensure the full involvement of the UK automotive industry in these developments.

The report established two quantitative targets: *i)* by 2012, 10% of all new car sales will emit 100 g per km of CO_2 or less at the tailpipe, and *ii)* by 2012, 600 or more buses coming into operation each year will have emissions 30% below current averages. A 2005 report on the transport strategy noted some progress towards meeting these goals but warned that substantial work remained to be done. Although average fuel efficiency continues to improve, cars emitting 120 g/km CO_2 or less accounted for just 3.2% of total new car sales in 2004, and a total of only 481 cars with less than 100 g/km CO_2 emissions were sold in the same year.

The government uses a number of policy tools to encourage greater transport efficiency. The Vehicle Excise Duty (VED) and Company Car Tax systems are both structured to reward those who purchase the most fuel-efficient vehicles. The 2006 Budget announced changes in the VED that gave even greater incentives to purchase fuel-efficient vehicles (see section on Energy Taxation in Chapter 3 for details). In addition, UK motor vehicle fuel taxes are among the highest in the world, although the 2006 Budget deferred the inflation-based increase in main road fuel duties until 1 September 2006. This deferral was in response to recently high and volatile prices in the oil and oil products markets.

A colour-coded energy efficiency labelling scheme for new cars was introduced in July 2005. This programme, the result of a voluntary agreement with the automotive industry, was introduced for all 42 UK car brands between July and September 2005. The label will help car buyers assess the climate change impacts of different cars. The label will also show how car buyers can cut their running costs if they buy a lower-carbon car. The new fuel economy label is intended to be familiar to consumers as it mirrors important aspects of the design and colour-coding of the energy efficiency labels that now appear on most "white goods", such as refrigerators. The gradations on the label are also consistent with the CO_2 bandings used for VED.

The government has also funded a number of programmes to minimise the impact of freight on the environment. These have included rail and water freight grants, which aim to transfer freight traffic from roads to these modes, and programmes to promote more efficient road haulage. In January 2006, the government also launched a GBP 1.3 million Safe and Fuel Efficient Drivers (SaFED) scheme, which is funding 200 instructors to offer training on advanced driving techniques to 3 500 van drivers across the country.

The government is considering the role that road pricing could play in reducing congestion, and will be supporting the development of a number of pilot schemes in local authority areas. These ideas were laid out in the Department of Transport's July 2004 White Paper, *Future of Transport: A Network for 2030*. This report also summarises the government's other policies in areas such as support for public transport, and improving the efficiency of our current transport infrastructure.

In February 2003, the City of London introduced a "congestion charge". A daily fee of GBP 8 must be paid by the registered owner of a vehicle that enters, leaves or moves around within the congestion charge zone between 7am and 6.30pm, Monday to Friday. Some vehicles, such as buses, minibuses (over a certain size), taxis, emergency service vehicles (*i.e.* ambulances, fire engines and police vehicles), motorcycles, alternative-fuel vehicles and bicycles are exempt from the charge. In September 2005, the city confirmed that the congestion zone would be expanded westward, a change that will come into effect in February 2007.

CRITIQUE

The UK government puts very high emphasis on energy efficiency, noting in the 2003 Energy White Paper that it is "the cheapest and safest way" of addressing their energy policy objectives. This approach has been reiterated in numerous other policy documents and statement by policy-makers. The IEA team commends the UK's focus on the demand side as a crucial component for sound energy policies. Many other IEA countries are also finding that demand reduction is often the most cost-effective way of ensuring energy security, reducing emissions and improving national competitiveness.

Unlike many other IEA countries where both energy supply and demand side are handled by the energy ministries, energy efficiency policy in the UK is the responsibility of Defra. Owing largely to this organisational arrangement, energy efficiency policies are largely driven by climate change mitigation. For example, efficiency targets are almost always stated in MtC of emissions reduction rather than in units of energy (*e.g.* kWh, tonnes of coal, or therms of gas). Given the multi-faceted role of energy efficiency as described above, close communication and co-ordination between Defra, DTI and other relevant bodies are essential so that energy efficiency policy can be pursued from broader energy and environment policy perspectives. This is particularly crucial in evaluating cost-effectiveness of policies and measures across energy demand and supply sides (e.g. energy efficiency and renewables). Enhanced energy security is one obvious benefit of efficiency beyond emissions reduction. At a time when energy security is receiving increased attention in the UK, greater appreciation of efficiency's contribution in this area could be helpful in shaping future policy.

Defra has implemented a wide range of energy efficiency policies and measures in the household, business and public sectors based on *Energy Efficiency: the Government's Plan for Action* in April 2004. While such a wide range of measures and programmes may lead to complications, dispersion of resources and occasional bureaucratic infighting, it also allows each programme to specialise in a particular area and to operate more independently and, ideally, more effectively. The UK government manages this inherent tension well. The wide range of measures also makes comparing the cost-effectiveness of each measure more difficult although the government has taken steps to address this problem through a Defra study released in April 2006.[21] Conclusions in the Defra study mirror similar analyses done in other countries, namely that efficiency and demand reduction measures generally offer more cost-effective solutions than supply-side measures. This validates the UK's focus on the demand side as a sound strategy. The government is encouraged to expand on such cost-effectiveness analysis and, more importantly, use it to determine the proper allocation of resources.

A major policy pillar in the household sector is the Energy Efficiency Commitment (EEC), which was put in place in 2002. Under the EEC, electricity and gas suppliers must achieve targets for the energy efficiency improvements in the household sector. In principle, suppliers can fulfil their obligations by carrying out any combination of approved measures, including installing insulation, supplying low-energy light bulbs, high-efficiency appliances and boilers. Given that energy consumption of the residential/commercial sector is continuously growing in many IEA countries, this instrument addressing the household sector, which is not subject to a Climate Change Levy or EU-ETS, is innovative and highly successful. In the first phase (2002-2005), energy suppliers surpassed their targets with net benefits. The programme's success can be attributed to various factors. First, putting obligations on a limited number of energy suppliers instead of numerous end-users has made the system management relatively simple. Second, the calculation of energy savings has been relatively easy because the measures have focused on insulation, heating, appliances and lighting. Ofgem published a list of all pre-

---

21. *Synthesis of Climate Change Policy Evaluations*, Department for Environment, Food and Rural Affairs (Defra), April 2006. Discussed more in Chapter 4.

approved measures that the suppliers may implement and how much energy savings each measure will be worth. This substantially lightens the administrative load for everyone involved. Third, there have been plenty of "low hanging fruit" for achieving the targets. The majority of the targets have been achieved through insulation, an area where UK housing has traditionally been poor. Fourth, there have been various initiatives by the Energy Saving Trust involving consumers and manufacturers/retailers of energy-efficient equipment to supplement the EEC.

These are all commendable and it is understandable that the government doubled the target for the second phase (2005-2008) and indicated its broad ambition for a further increase in the coming third phase (2008-2011). Having said that, there are several challenges to be addressed. First, given that low hanging fruit will be gradually exploited, broader measures, such as microgeneration, behavioural changes and smart metering will need to be incorporated. In the mid to long term, EEC can be utilised to encourage innovative low-carbon technologies, which are essential in achieving the government's long-term target of 60% emissions reduction in 2050. In fact, the government is already moving in this direction, with the Climate Change and Sustainable Energy Act of 2006 allowing microgeneration and other measures affecting consumer behaviour to be included in the EEC. Also, the government and Ofgem should ensure that such a wider scope will not result in unduly complicated and cumbersome administrative procedures. Energy suppliers already must devote administrative efforts to comply with their obligations with the current limited range of measures. It is a challenging task to broaden the scope while minimising administrative burdens. For this purpose, developing standardised and simple methodology for calculating energy savings from any newly introduced measures is essential

The government may consider additional measures for changing the behaviour of the household sector together with incorporating broader measures in the EEC. Certain UK actors have suggested that there could be a tax incentive (*e.g.* reduction in community tax) for a reduction in energy consumption. While ensuring that policies targeted on end-users and those targeted on energy suppliers would not hamper their overall efficiency and effectiveness, such options would merit consideration.

In addition, the efficacy of incorporating social policy objectives in EEC should be carefully evaluated. Currently, energy suppliers must realise at least half of their energy savings in the priority sector (*i.e.* low-income households). However, imposing such constraints likely reduces the overall cost-effectiveness of the system. In fact, it is likely that suppliers could realise savings at a lower cost in wealthier households since such end-users would be able to pay for a greater share of the measures put in place. Putting consumer contributions aside, any type of restrictions put on the suppliers will raise the cost of the entire system. There is, of course, an equity issue to be considered.

Since all consumers contribute equally to the cost of the EEC (through higher energy rates), supplier activity heavily weighted towards upper-income customers would result in an implicit subsidy from the less well-off to the better-off. In addition, lifting the 50% obligation for the priority sector would diminish the EEC's effectiveness as a tool for combating fuel poverty. The EEC was launched as an energy efficiency programme and the 50% requirement could hamper its ability to achieve its goals. While equity and fuel poverty are important policy issues, they can be pursued more effectively through more direct and targeted policies that are not incorporated in the EEC programme itself. This issue is among those being considered in an early government consultation to help shape EEC3 and prepare for the formal consultation in 2007.

Certain UK actors have suggested that this system be transformed to a cap and trade mechanism with tradable White Certificates. This could make it more market-oriented. A potential risk is that such a system may be administratively more complicated. Given that France and Italy are introducing a White Certificate scheme, and that Denmark is introducing a related scheme, the government should carefully examine the experiences in these countries and explore its feasibility. The UK government set out its early thinking in the Energy Review and intends to look at a cap and trade mechanism in the form of a Supplier Obligation, which would stimulate suppliers to move towards an energy services approach rather than just the provision of energy.

Building codes are another strong measure in the household sector. It is encouraging that the new and stronger building codes, which will enhance energy efficiency for new building up from 18% to 27%, have been put in place from April 2006. In Denmark, where building codes have been highly successful in promoting energy efficiency, the government regularly announces how the building codes will be strengthened in the coming years. This gives certainty to the building and housing industries and enables them to prepare for any changes. The UK government is developing the Code for Sustainable Homes (levels 1 to 5). Such codes should have indicative time frames as to when each level will be put in place as a mandatory code. It is a cause of concern that the compliance level of the building code is low. Experience with the previous code shows that one-third to one-half of all new buildings did not meet the relevant regulations. Stronger leadership by the government is required. This could include enhancing awareness and capacity building (more staffing and training) with the local authorities enforcing building regulations. In addition, there can be difficulties in obtaining adequate, transparent data on energy efficiency in the household sector. This appears to result at least in part from the division of responsibilities among Defra, DTI and the Office of the Deputy Prime Minister. Greater co-ordination in gathering and disseminating data could help both policy makers and industry. The Energy Review report recognises the need for enforcing building codes and outlines a number of steps it has taken and will take to improve the situation.

Improving the energy efficiency of large non energy-intensive industries and small and medium-sized enterprises (SMEs) is a challenge. The household sector has the EEC, as well as fuel poverty programmes for the disadvantaged, and the energy-intensive users have the CCL, Climate Change Agreements (CCAs) and the EU-ETS but there are fewer programmes for medium-size consumers. Increasing government efforts to fit energy users that fall between these two groups could be a cost-effective way to reduce demand. The Carbon Trust has proposed development of a new emissions trading scheme for large non energy-intensive industries and expansion of the EEC to SMEs. The Energy Review 2006 appears to favour the emissions trading option. The Review proposes an Energy Performance Commitment whereby some 5 000 organisations such as supermarket chains, hotel chains and government departments are required to participate in such a scheme. Consultations and final decisions are expected in the first half of 2007. We caution the government to the complexity of such a trading scheme, especially since the participants will be much smaller than those in the EU-ETS and will have less expertise and resources to devote to trading emissions. The expansion of the EEC to SMEs should remain a possibility in the consultations. While this would also raise the administrative burden for participants and government, the success of the EEC in minimising such costs so far suggests that these challenges could be overcome.

Another solution could be to expand the scope of CCAs to non energy-intensive industries and SMEs. In this case, the CCL, which small firms do not currently pay, may also need to be extended to them in order to encourage them to join CCAs. Political resistance may be overcome by ensuring revenue-neutrality. A programme in the Netherlands, LTA2, represents a good example of voluntary agreements with non energy-intensive industries and SMEs. Small companies can collectively join LTA2 if they have a total energy consumption of at least one petajoule per year. Each participating company has to draw up an Energy Conservation Plan, which sets an efficiency target, proposes specific measures and establishes a schedule for their implementation. NOVEM, which is equivalent to the Carbon Trust, monitors the progress of LTA2 and receives annual progress reports from the participants. The government should carefully examine various options for capturing energy efficiency potential in the non energy-intensive industries and SMEs.

The transport sector has the highest rate of energy growth in the UK. While the government, largely through the Department of Transport, has a number of programmes to address transport energy demand, these efforts are not as substantial as those found in other sectors. In fact, efficiency transport measures at the Energy Savings Trust have recently been curtailed. To be fair, almost all IEA countries are having difficulty in addressing energy use in their transport sectors. Certainly the structure of the VED whereby less efficient vehicles face a higher tax is one way to promote efficiency, and the recent budget announcement that the VED will be further graduated is welcome. Nevertheless, the sums involved remain minor and therefore unlikely to have a great effect. For example, the introduction of a higher band of VED for the least efficient cars set at GBP 210 will only sway a small number of car buyers when considering the purchase of a vehicle that already costs tens of thousands of pounds. In addition, shielding customers from high and/or volatile oil prices by deferring agreed-upon, inflation-based tax increases – in effect lowering the real level of the tax – acts to increase transport demand at the exact time it should be reduced via a market response to price pressures.

The congestion charge in London is an innovative approach to traffic management. While not intended primarily as a means of curbing transport energy use, it does make operating a motor vehicle more costly and thus encourages environment-friendly travel such as public transport and bicycles. This provides a good example for other countries, a number of which are looking into similar programmes. While such congestion zones only make sense in large urban areas and their impact would be minimal on a national scale, the congestion zone nevertheless shows how transport projects aimed at easing traffic flow and improving quality of life can, and normally do, also reduce energy demand. In this way, reducing transport demand should very much be a goal in all transport planning such as the DfT's activities related to its 2004 White Paper, *Future of Transport: A Network for 2030*.

RECOMMENDATIONS

The government of the United Kingdom should:

▶ *Ensure that energy efficiency policies will be pursued not only from a climate change perspective but also from broader energy policy perspectives, including security of supply concerns, through close co-ordination between Defra and DTI.*

▶ *Expand the cost-effectiveness analysis of energy efficiency policies and reflect the outcome in the portfolio of efficiency measures.*

▶ *Further improve the EEC by incorporating a wider range of measures, with the scope of promoting innovative energy efficiency technologies, while striving to simplify administrative procedures as much as possible through developing standardised methodology for calculating energy savings.*

▶ *Consider a tax incentive for households to supplement the effectiveness of the EEC.*

- *Reconsider the effect of ring-fencing 50% of EEC investment for priority groups on the overall cost-effectiveness of the programme and compare this with more direct and targeted measures to reduce fuel poverty.*

- *Examine experiences of White Certificate schemes in other countries and consider the feasibility of such a scheme in the UK.*

- *Increase predictability of future development of building codes, for example through advanced notice of proposed changes. Consider a time frame to incorporate the Code of Sustainable Homes in the building code.*

- *Improve enforcement of the building code by local authorities.*

- *Enhance the availability and quality of energy efficiency data in the household sector.*

- *Look for ways to fully include non energy-intensive industry and SMEs in the government's efficiency efforts, for example by expanding the EEC to allow suppliers to realise savings in the commercial sector, or by expanding the scope of CCAs.*

- *Take appropriate measures to capture energy efficiency potential in the sectors not covered by EU-ETS, CCA or EEC.*

- *Pursue additional means of curbing transport energy demand, and consider taxation, integration of demand concerns in a larger transport planning framework and other measures.*

CURRENT AND HISTORICAL PRODUCTION

The UK has modest natural resources for hydropower, biomass or solar energy although it does have an excellent wind profile and a long coastline for wave and tidal energy. In 2004, renewables accounted for just 1.6% of TPES, the second-lowest figure in the OECD. By far the largest share of renewable energy came from biomass which accounted for 1.3% of TPES. This was followed by hydropower (0.2% of TPES), wind power (0.07%) and solar thermal energy (0.01%). Despite these modest levels, renewable energy has seen rapid growth rates in recent years. From 1990 to 2004, renewables grew by more than 240% (annual rate of 9.2%) and from 2000 to 2004, renewables grew by more than 50% (10.6% annually). By way of comparison, the UK TPES for all fuels grew at an average annual rate of 0.7% from 1990 to 2004.

Renewables play a slightly larger role in power generation. In 2004, total electricity generation from renewable resources was 3.8% of the total with 2.0% coming from biomass, 1.3% from hydropower and 0.5% from wind. The share for 2005 is 4% although the breakdown by technology is not available. Renewables' share of total power generation has risen from 1.9% in 1990 and from 1.8% in 2002 when the Renewables Obligation (see below) was introduced. In 2004, 240 MW of new wind capacity was built, in 2005 446 MW and, for the first eight months of 2006, 601 MW. There is a further 329 MW under construction. In January 2006, construction of a 44 MW biomass plant, the largest in the UK, was begun.

The UK government projects that renewable energy production will expand substantially in the coming years. From the 2004 level of 1.6% of TPES, renewables are expected to account for 4.3% in 2010 and 6.1% in 2020. Biomass is expected to see the greatest absolute growth, increasing its contribution by 9.8 Mtoe between 2004 and 2020, or more than 400%. Wind is projected to have the greatest percentage growth with an increase of nearly 700% from 2004 to 2020. For electricity generation, renewable energy is projected to account for 13.4% of the total by 2020. These projections may in fact underestimate the actual level of renewables realised if government support mechanisms, as described below, achieve their intended targets.

GOVERNMENT SUPPORT PROGRAMMES

The Renewables Obligation is the government's main mechanism for supporting renewable energy. Introduced in April 2002, it provides a market

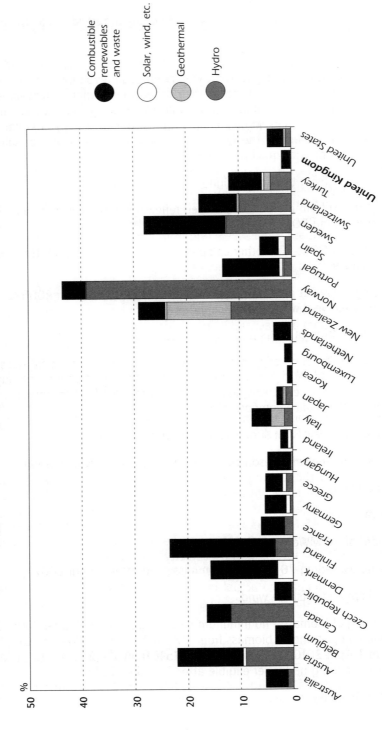

Figure 11

Renewable Energy as a Percentage of Total Primary Energy Supply in IEA Countries, 2005*

Combustible renewables and waste

Solar, wind, etc.

Geothermal

Hydro

* estimates.

Source: Energy Balances of OECD Countries, IEA/OECD Paris, 2006.

incentive for all eligible forms of renewable energy. In Scotland, the Scottish Renewables Obligation is in place. A Northern Ireland Renewables Obligation was introduced on 1 April 2005.

The Obligation is enforced by an Order (statutory instrument) made under the terms of the Utilities Act 2000. The Obligation requires suppliers to source an annually increasing percentage of their sales from eligible renewables. For each megawatt-hour of eligible renewable electricity generated, a tradable certificate called a Renewables Obligation Certificate (ROC) is issued. The generator can either use the ROC itself (if it is also a supplier) or sell it to another supplier, with or without electricity.

Suppliers can meet their obligation by:

- Generating from their directly owned renewable resources and gaining the corresponding ROCs.

- Purchasing ROCs from other companies at prices and terms determined by the market.

- Paying a buy-out price equivalent to GBP 33.24 per MWh for 2006/07 and rising each year with retail price index.

- A combination of ROCs and paying a buy-out price.

When a supplier chooses to pay the buy-out price, the money paid goes into the buy-out fund. At the end of the 12-month Obligation period, the buy-out fund is recycled to electricity suppliers presenting ROCS in proportion to the number of ROCs each company presents.

The obligation levels for suppliers are shown in Table 17.

Only certain renewable resources are eligible under the RO. These are:

- Landfill gas.

- Sewage gas.

- Hydro of 20 MWe net or less.

- Hydro exceeding 20 MWe net commissioned after 1 April 2002.

- Onshore and offshore wind.

- Co-firing of biomass – no minimum percentage until 31 March 2009, 25% minimum co-firing of biomass from 1 April 2009 to 31 March 2010, 50% from 1 April 2010 to 31 March 2011, 75% from 1 April 2011 to 31 March 2016. Co-firing no longer eligible after 31 March 2016.

- Other biomass.

Supplier Obligation Levels for Renewables Obligation (RO)

Obligation period[1]	% of electricity supplies
2006/07	6.7
2007/08	7.9
2008/09	9.1
2009/10	9.7
2010/11	10.4
2011/12	11.4
2012/13	12.4
2013/14	13.4
2014/15	14.4
2015/16	15.4
up to 2027	15.4

1. Each period starts 1 April.

Source: DTI.

- Geothermal power.

- Tidal and wave power.

- Photovoltaics.

As a group, suppliers required to acquire Renewables Obligation Certificates (ROCs) have failed to meet their obligations each of the years the RO has been in place. Table 18 shows information on compliance.

Looking on supplier-by-supplier compliance levels, significantly less than 50% of obligated companies have been in compliance, with the remainder meeting their requirement through a combination of ROCs and buy-outs or completely with buy-outs. Of the compliant suppliers, some met their obligation fully with ROCs from their own generating stations while others mixed their own ROCs and ROCs purchased from other renewables generators. In 2005, eligible RO generation was 4% compared to the obligation level of 5.5%.

The price of traded ROCs is currently in the GBP 40 per MWh range. This is higher than buy-out price (GBP 33.24 per MWh for 2006/07) due to the buy-out fund flowing back to suppliers in proportion to the number of ROCs they

——————————————————— Table **18**

Compliance of Obligated Suppliers under the RO

Year	ROCs submitted	ROCs required	Aggregate compliance rate	Number of eligible suppliers	Number of suppliers compliant	% of compliant suppliers
2004/05	14 315 784	20 747 513	69%	n/a	8	n/a
2003/04	12 387 720	22 120 929	56%	40	10	25%
2002/03	5 562 669	9 428 253	59%	38	12	32%

Source: Ofgem.

have submitted. Prices at a popular auction website have been falling: GBP 48 in July 2003; GBP 52 in July 2004; GBP 45 in July 2005; and GBP 40 in July 2006.

For the most recent period for which final figures exist (2004/05), the largest share of ROCs came from landfill gas plants with 33.6% of the total. The figure below shows the breakdown of all ROCs by technology.

——————————————————— Figure **12**

Renewables Obligation Certificates Issued by Technology Type, 2004/05

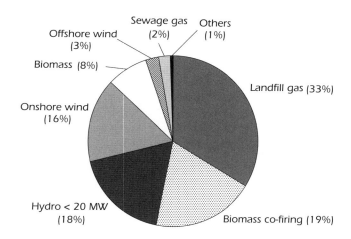

Source: Ofgem.

Energy Review and the RO

The Energy Review report of July 2006 discussed several aspects of the RO. While many of its proposals had not been finalised or decided, it did outline a number of measures intended to improve the programme's operation. These include:

- Maintaining obligation levels above the level of actual ROC-eligible renewable generation, up to a maximum of 20% of generation.

- Removing the automatic increases of the buy-out price with inflation from 2015 onward.

- Removing the risk of unanticipated oversupply of ROCs in any one period and consequent decrease in ROC prices.

- "Banding" by technology whereby lesser developed technologies receive more ROCs per MWh generated, thus further encouraging their use and helping them gain competitiveness.

- Streamlining the planning process for new renewable generating plants.

RENEWABLE ENERGY TECHNOLOGIES

ONSHORE WIND

The UK has one of the best wind profiles in Europe. There are currently 123 onshore wind farms in operation accounting for a combined capacity of 1 481 MW. In addition, there are 21 new farms under construction with a combined capacity of 389 MW. Seventy-four projects have received planning permission and related consents. These projections have a combined capacity of 1 697 MW. Finally, 166 wind farms are in the planning stage. If fully realised, they would have a combined capacity of 6.7 GW, compared to the total electricity generating capacity for the UK (including autoproducers) of roughly 79 GW.

OFFSHORE WIND

In the first round of the UK offshore wind programme, 12 sites received consent, representing around 1 GW of capacity – sufficient to power around 600 000 homes. These projects all have planned commercial operating dates by 2010. The first large-scale offshore wind farm at North Hoyle (60 MW) was completed in November 2003; Scroby Sands (60 MW) was completed in December 2004 and Kentish Flats (90 MW) in September 2005. Round 1 projects, apart from being eligible under the Renewables Obligation, have already been allocated GBP 117 million by the DTI as capital grants. The amount of the grants offered to individual projects was around GBP 10 million per application, and this is roughly equivalent to the cost of grid connection to the distribution system. Applications for Site Lease and Exploration Licences for the second round of the offshore wind programme were allocated in 2003. The total generating capacity of wind farms proposed by applicants amounted to over 26 GW, more than three times the amount for which site leases could be offered.

BIOMASS

The Bioenergy Capital Grants Scheme was launched in February 2002. The GBP 66 million scheme, jointly funded by DTI and the National Lottery's New Opportunities Fund, was competitive and over-subscribed. Twenty-one bioenergy projects have been offered grants under the scheme, which range from the installation of heat cluster technology, combined heat and power (CHP), to larger-scale projects over 20 MW deploying state-of-the-art thermal combustion and advanced conversion technology.

Farmers in England can apply for establishment grants for energy crops through the GBP 29 million Energy Crops Scheme run by Defra. Grants range from GBP 920 for miscanthus to GBP 1 600 for short rotation coppice planted on ex-livestock land. Farmers and landowners in the rest of the UK can apply for more modest grants for the establishment of short rotation coppice through the Woodland Grants Scheme run by the Forestry Commission (Scotland/Wales) and Forest Services (Northern Ireland).

SOLAR PHOTOVOLTAIC (PV) POWER

Installed PV generating capacity increased in 2004 by 26% and currently the UK has an installed solar PV base of approximately 8.2 MW. Support for the development of solar PV technology ranges from encouraging innovation in research and development to stimulating the market for PV systems. This is being achieved through:

- GBP 10 million already committed through Domestic and Large Scale Field Trials for a diverse set of PV installations from homes to offices.

- Major Photovoltaics Demonstration Programme (PV MDP) with GBP 31 million of capital grants available from 2002 to 2006.

- Research and development (R&D) programme of GBP 2.5 million per annum and rising.

- Ministerial initiatives to encourage UK and foreign companies to invest in PV cell, module and system component manufacture in the UK.

BIOFUELS

The government currently supports biofuels for transport through incentives. In 2002, a 20p per litre reduction on tax was introduced for fuels containing biodiesel and in 2005, the same incentive was given to bioethanol. In 2004, sales of all biofuels combined were 20 million litres. This rose to 120 million litres in 2005 which was equivalent to 0.24% of total transport liquid fuels used in the UK.

The government plans to institute the Renewables Transport Fuel Obligation (RTFO) in April 2008. The RTFO places a legal obligation on transport fuel suppliers to make available a specified proportion of their road fuel supplies to their customers in the UK from renewable energy sources. This obligation will start at 2.5% in 2008, rising to 3.75% in 2009 and then 5% in 2010. Fuel suppliers who do not meet their obligation will have to pay a buy-out price of 15p per litre. This will be in addition to the 20p per litre tax incentives currently in place for biofuels and thus the effective support level will be 35p per litre.

CRITIQUE

While the UK has had historically low levels of renewable energy, current government support schemes are increasing renewables production substantially. While still modest, targets for renewable energy in the coming years would make renewables a major fuel source for the UK. This brings benefits in terms of GHG emissions reduction and enhanced energy security since renewables represent another domestic fuel source. Since emissions and security are the two major issues facing the UK energy sector, additional renewables production can provide substantial benefits.

The primary means of supporting renewables is the Renewables Obligation (RO). This market-oriented certificate scheme is intended to put competitive pressure on renewables suppliers, thus keeping the price down and encouraging further technology development. While the largest share of ROCs for the 2004/05 period came from landfill gas, suitable LFG sites are limited and most observers see the RO being dominated by onshore wind. However, the programme has been having some problems. Many suppliers do not comply with their obligations and aggregate compliance for all suppliers has only been between 50% and 65%, although this is rising. In addition, the price of ROCs is now in the neighbourhood of GBP 40 per ROC. While this price level actually represents a fall from previous years, it is still high by international standards.

This is not to say that the programme has not had success in bringing new renewable generation on line. While this has been less than expected, it is still substantial. In addition, it is much too early to pass summary judgements on the programme, especially given the lead times necessary to develop, finance, obtain planning permission, and construct a new generating station. While the higher prices for ROCs are undesirable in that they further increase costs to consumers, they are doing what the programme was intended for, which is to deliver a strong price signal for renewables to the market. Nevertheless, the RO faces important challenges going forward in two major areas:

- It is not yet generating the actual renewable generation it is intended to generate.

- It is not keeping the costs down for customers that end up paying the bill.

- It is significantly more expensive than energy efficiency, for the same amount of CO_2 avoided.

Eligible renewable generators receive the GBP 40 ROC value plus whatever price they can receive from the market for the electricity produced. This combined revenue is well above the long-range marginal cost of many renewable energy technologies, including onshore wind. In a recent report,[22] the European Commission assesses the UK as having among the lowest costs for onshore wind power along with some of the highest price supports. This report calculated that the cost of onshore wind was roughly between EUR 50 and 60 per MWh while the prices received for the electricity generated was between EUR 110 and 120 per kWh. In addition, in order to ensure that other currently less competitive technologies also receive the necessary support, the government has grant programmes. From 2002 to 2008, GBP 500 million of funding will be given to technologies such as offshore wind, biomass, solar energy, and wave and tidal power to supplement their income from ROCs and sales of electricity. The government should investigate which renewable sources, if any, are receiving oversubsidisation and thus making above-market rates of return on their investments due to the government support programmes.

The current problems should not be regarded as peculiar to a quota obligation scheme. Utilisation of market-based instruments to promote renewables is, in itself, a commendable approach. In a perfect market situation, the high ROC prices would yield a supply response and, therefore, ROC prices would decrease to a competitive level. In fact, Australia has a certificate scheme with prices substantially lower than currently seen in the UK. While there are important differences between the two countries, the UK government should nevertheless look to Australia for examples of best practice. Sweden also provides a good example of a successful renewables certificates scheme. The aforementioned Commission report estimates that costs for onshore wind and the support levels are very close (around EUR 60 per MWh). This indicates that

---

22. *The support of electricity from renewable energy sources.* Commission of the European Communities, 7 December 2005.

competition is placing support at the proper level and promoting efficient operation. The government is encouraged to look at other countries where renewables certificate schemes, or simply renewables schemes in general, have had success in stimulating renewables in a cost-effective manner.

The biggest problem in the UK comes from difficulties in gaining the necessary planning permissions and consents to achieve the target. Many investors wishing to expand their renewables generation to take advantage of the high ROC prices have not been able to actually construct the plants. The government is advised to look into this issue very carefully. Local communities can, and should, have permitting authority for new facilities. However, since these facilities have a benefit for the country as a whole, the UK government has a role in ensuring that permitting is not unduly delayed. Regarding the difficulty with siting, the government could look to Denmark, which has added a much higher percentage of wind turbines than the UK is forecasting, and has had fewer difficulties with local opposition to siting. One reason for this is that local communities, landowners and farmers have been included as equity participants in the wind turbines constructed.

The government has also launched a programme to support biofuels for the transport sector. In addition to current and ongoing tax incentives, the government will soon be launching a certificates obligation scheme for all motor fuel suppliers whereby 5% of the fuels they sell by 2010 must be biofuels. The price of these certificates will be capped at 15p per litre which, in combination with the 20p per litre tax incentive, would be a total possible support of 35p per litre for biofuels. This is considered well above the support level needed to make biofuels competitive at current world oil prices. It also raises questions about whether such subsidies are a cost-effective way to achieve benefits from renewables. The government is encouraged to examine more fully the cost and benefits of government support for biofuels.

RECOMMENDATIONS

The government of the United Kingdom should:

▶ *Check for oversubsidisation of renewable energy technologies receiving high prices for Renewables Obligation Certificates (ROCs) and electricity prices as well as capital grants or other schemes.*

▶ *Look for lessons from other countries where renewables certificate schemes have achieved desired compliance rates at costs below current UK conditions.*

▶ *Examine more fully the costs and benefits of biofuels, including accurate assessments of carbon savings and benefits to national and global supply security coming from decreased oil demand.*

GENERAL ELECTRICITY POLICY

Since 1990, the UK electricity sector has gone through a remarkable process of unbundling, wide-scale privatisation and introduction of competition. The reforms allowed the sector rapidly to transform the portfolio of generation technologies to take advantage of relatively cheap domestic and imported natural gas and replace relatively old and inefficient coal-fired stations. Labour productivity improved without jeopardising system security. Consumers have been given a real choice of supplier and products. Liberalisation and competition have set the scene in electricity policy in the UK for almost two decades.

The Electricity Pool of England & Wales (the Pool) was established in April 1990 to direct wholesale pricing and trading of electricity. The Pool was an obligatory trading arrangement that calculated dispatch, remunerations and charges. Active government and regulatory involvement transformed the structure of the sector to become increasingly competitive. After the first phase of market opening, competition steadily improved but problems in the trading mechanism and in the governing structures had also arisen. The new Labour government launched a process to reform the Pool in 1997 and in 2001 it was replaced with the New Electricity Trading Arrangements (NETA). NETA is a much looser trading platform that allows market participants more freedom to make bilateral trading arrangements and contracts. NETA only co-ordinates actions during the last hours allowing the system operator to operate and balance the system efficiently and securely.

A new Utilities Act 2000 was passed in July 2000 to prepare the ground for NETA and to merge the gas and electricity regulators into one body: the Office of Gas and Electricity Markets (Ofgem). The subsequent Energy Act 2004 led to the integration of the wholesale electricity market in Great Britain. NETA was extended to Scotland in April 2005 in the form of the British Electricity Trading and Transmission Arrangements (BETTA).

Northern Ireland was not included in the new trading arrangements but the sector has also been privatised and competition has been introduced as required by EU directives. The 1 000 largest consumers have been free to choose their supplier since 2000. In November 2004, ministers in Ireland and Northern Ireland signed a framework document outlining a path towards an all-island electricity market. Regulatory authorities later signed a memorandum of understanding with a commitment to launch the market no later than 1 July 2007.

The UK governments' Energy White Paper of 2003 did not depart from the dedication to markets as an instrument to ensure good performance. However, it did bring additional focus on energy security and the impacts on climate change, notably targeting a 60% reduction in carbon emissions by 2050. Increased shares of renewable energy, other small-scale generation and greater contributions from natural gas were seen as the main contributors in the electricity sector. New nuclear power was not ruled out but deemed less cost-effective than these other options at the time. With the 2006 Energy Review, nuclear power received renewed attention.

ELECTRICITY SUPPLY AND DEMAND

SUPPLY

Since 1973, the generation mix has undergone two major shifts. In the first phase until 1990, the share supplied from nuclear power increased from 10% to 21%, displacing oil-fired generation which decreased from 26% to 11%. The second phase (1990 to present) was notable for the replacement of coal-fired generation with gas-fired generation. The share of coal-fired generation stayed relatively constant from 1973 to 1990, but from 1990 to 2003 it decreased from 65% to 35%. Over the same period, gas-fired generation increased from 2% to 38%. The last ten years are also characterised by less stable shares of natural gas and coal, often changing substantially from year to year. This is due to the fact that coal and gas use for power generation responds dynamically to the relative prices of gas and coal.

The fuel mix in UK electricity generation has been more diverse during the last decade compared to the previous very strong reliance on coal. DTI projections of the fuel mix until 2020 show a further increase in the natural gas share reaching 61% in 2020. Combustible renewables and waste, and other renewable sources are projected to make up for the loss of ageing nuclear power plants, increasing to a share of 13% in 2020.

The transformation of the UK electricity system since 1990, and the emergence of gas-fired plant as an important contributor, is even more marked in terms of installed capacity. From 1990 to 1994, 14 GW of combustible generating capacity (excluding combined-cycle gas turbines, CCGTs) were decommissioned. This was replaced with 9 GW of CCGT by 1994 and 27 GW by 2004. An additional 7 GW of combustible generating capacity, excluding CCGT, was decommissioned by 2004. Owing to the EU directive limiting emissions for large combustion plants, 8 GW of coal-fired generating capacity will, according to DTI, have to close in the period from 2008 to 2015. Existing nuclear capacity is ageing, and 8 GW or two-thirds of the installed nuclear capacity is planned to be decommissioned between 2006 and 2014, even if the prospects for extending the lifetimes of some capacity is being

Figure **13**

Electricity Generation by Source, 1973 to 2020

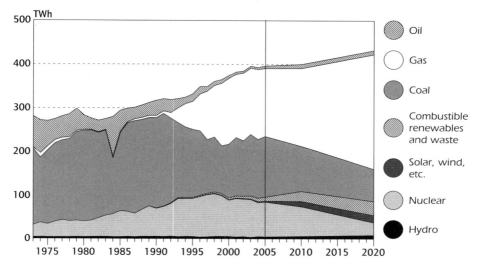

Sources: *Energy Balances of OECD Countries*, IEA/OECD Paris, 2006 and country submission.

reconsidered at the moment. This implies the loss of up to 16 GW or more of installed generating capacity by 2015, corresponding to 20% of total current capacity. More than 15 GW of coal and nuclear generating capacity was installed before 1980 and is over 25 years old. A part of this capacity should be retired by 2015-2020, but market players have announced plans to invest in flue gas desulphurisation (FGD) equipment to extend the lifetime of 9 GW of coal-fired generation. Until 2005/06 nearly 4 GW of coal-fired stations had FGD equipment installed.

Total installed generating capacity has increased with the pace of peak demand. Since 1990, there have been years where the margin of installed capacity over peak demand was lower, but generally, the initial trading arrangements in the Pool and the current trading arrangements in NETA/BETTA have sufficiently encouraged new generating capacity.[23] The 2-GW interconnector between the UK and France also contributes to reserve margin and security of supply, representing about 3.3% of peak UK demand.

---

23. The Pool gave a specific remuneration for generating capacity through the capacity payment. Abandoning the remuneration does not seem to have affected the plant margin greatly so far. However, it is still difficult to draw firm conclusions on the capacity payments effects, given long lead times for plant development and construction and the many other factors affecting the reserve margin.

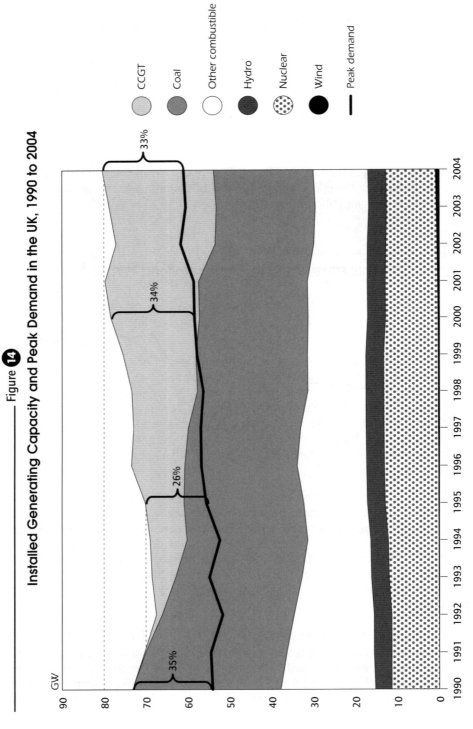

Figure 14

Installed Generating Capacity and Peak Demand in the UK, 1990 to 2004

Sources: International Energy Agency and the Department of Trade and Industry.

The National Grid expects 12 600 MW of new capacity to come on line by 2010, including 6.4 GW of CCGT, 7.2 GW of wind power and an 800-MW interconnector with the Netherlands.

Another marked change is seen in the utilisation of conventional coal-fired stations. Figure 15 shows the development of thermal efficiency since 1970 which is a measure of the level of energy output per unit of energy input. The development shows a gradual yet significant improvement in thermal efficiency from 1970 to 2002. Replacement of older stations with new, more advanced stations throughout this period is an important driver. There is a step change upwards from 1992 to 1993. This coincides with the commissioning of the first significant share of CCGTs shifting out old coal-fired plants and with the end of the three years of vesting contracts smoothing the transition to competition from market launch in 1990.

—————————————————— Figure **15**

Thermal Efficiency of Coal-fired Stations, 1970 to 2004

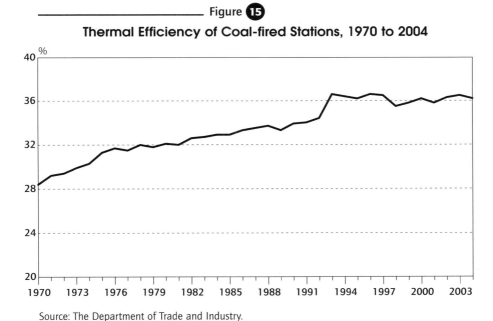

Source: The Department of Trade and Industry.

DEMAND

UK electricity demand has increased by almost 50% during the last 20 years. Industrial consumption has seen the lowest average annual growth rates, even with negative average growth rates from 1974 to 1980. Industrial consumption was just below 50% of total electricity consumption in 1960, a share which has been falling to the current share of less than 35%. Consumption from commercial, public services and agriculture only had a share of around 15% in 1960 but has increased to just below 30% today. The share of this sector particularly increased from 1974 to 1983. Residential consumption represents roughly the same share of total consumption as industrial consumption. Electricity demand peaks during winter time, and in 2004 the demand peak for the UK was 61 GW.

Final Consumption of Electricity by Sector, 1973 to 2020

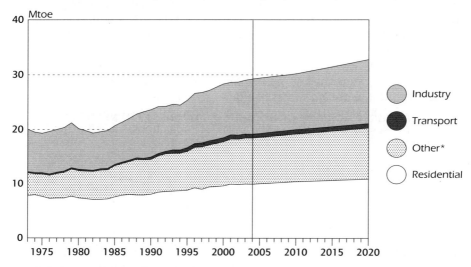

* includes commercial, public service and agricultural sectors.
Sources: *Energy Balances of OECD Countries*, IEA/OECD Paris, 2006 and country submission.

Encouraging consumers to respond to price by shifting demand during periods of relative tight supply-demand balance is seen as a very important element of a robust market. Such demand response can limit market power and provide a cost-efficient resource. Demand response is also a priority in the British market, and the move away from the supply-focused Pool to the truly two-sided trading arrangements in BETTA has contributed to this. The greatest impact from demand response is in the market for operational reserves and other ancillary services organised by the National Grid, allowing them to operate the system at the required reliability level. The National Grid has successfully allowed the demand side to bid into this market and in 2005 they had committed more than 4 GW of demand to respond in various different ways. It has additionally been observed that 800 MW of demand has responded to the market price during situations with tight supply and demand balance.

SUPPLY-DEMAND PROJECTIONS

Every year, the transmission system operator (National Grid) publishes a report projecting generation supply, consumer demand and the use of transmission infrastructure for the coming seven years. This report, entitled the *GB Seven Year Statement (SYS)*, is a tool to disseminate information and analysis, thereby improving the possibility for market players to respond appropriately to the needs of the market.

The point of reference for the report is the system's ability to meet peak demand in average cold spell (ACS) conditions. For the *2005 Statement*, the winter of 2005/06 ACS was estimated at 62.4 GW, while actual peak demand was 60.3 GW, or 2.1 GW lower than projected in the base scenario. The methodology used in the seven-year statement includes both forecasts based on input from market participants and the National Grid's own forecast. The National Grid's latest update of base case scenario projects a growth in ACS through 2012/13 to 68.4 GW. This is 0.6 GW higher than the 67.8 GW peak they calculate on the basis of projections from the market participants.

The projection of generation available to meet demand is based on existing installed capacity, formally notified decommissioning of capacity and new generation projects that have entered into a bilateral agreement with the National Grid about connection to the transmission system. The 2006 seven-year statement of generating capacity projects that generation and import capacity will see a net increase of 18.2 GW by 2012/13. The largest contributor to increases is new CCGT and new wind power, and the largest contributor to decreases is the decommissioning of the old Magnox nuclear power plants. These data do not include possible expansion in embedded generation resources such as micro-CHP. With the update in August 2006, the projection was adjusted upwards with an additional 8.1 GW by 2012/13.

The National Grid notes that the total plant margin to meet ACS will depend on the demand scenario, and on the fact that new generating capacity may not develop as projected, even if it has been contracted to connect to the grid. Availability of generating capacity is also an important issue, particularly in the light of the increasing share of wind power. The seven-year statement presents projections for plant margins under different assumptions and different scenarios. Assuming that only existing plants and plants under construction will be available in 2012/13, there is still a margin of more than 10% above the user-based high-demand growth scenario. Including the contracted generating capacity, the plant margin increased to almost 40% in the National Grid's demand growth scenario. This would, however, also include a larger share of wind power whose availability is dependent on meteorological conditions.

Generation plant margins do not seem to be a great concern over the next seven years, but the National Grid has also pointed out that a seven-year framework may not be appropriate for analysis in the current situation where substantial decommissioning is expected after 2012/13. The fact that new coal and nuclear plants are again more likely options and that the planning and construction horizon for these technologies are longer than seven years also emphasise the need for longer projections, *e.g.* ten years as the National Grid does for its natural gas forecasts.

The SYS also makes projections of the use of transmission assets, and these projections raise more reasons for concern. There are at present some bottlenecks in the system, and these are projected to be more severe, particularly with the development of wind power in the north.

INDUSTRY STRUCTURE

The structure of Great Britain's (GB) electricity sector started a fundamental transformation in 1990 with the Electricity Act 1989 triggering a process of unbundling and privatisation. Prior to the reform, generation and transmission in England and Wales were managed in the Central Electric Generating Board (CEGB), while distribution and supply were managed in 12 regional electricity boards. Everything was state-owned. Today the entire sector is privately-owned, apart from the 1.9 GW of nuclear Magnox power stations.

GENERATION

Three generation companies were formed in England and Wales in the initial restructuring of 1990: National Power with 29.7 GW conventional generating capacity, Power Gen with 18.7 GW of conventional capacity and Nuclear Electric (today British Energy's nuclear power stations in England and Wales) with 8.8 GW of mostly nuclear generating capacity. Three companies were also created in Scotland: Scottish Power (based on the vertically integrated former South of Scotland Electricity Board), Scottish Hydro-Electric (previously the vertically integrated North of Scotland Hydro-Electric Board) and Scottish Nuclear (which owned the Torness and Hunterston B nuclear power stations that are now British Energy assets). The very rapid transformation of the generation portfolio also implied a wide range of newcomers in the generation market. Some divestitures by the largest initial generation companies throughout the 1990s further fragmented the ownership of generation assets. The last important step towards fragmentation took place in 1999/2000, prior to the launch of NETA. Since then, some consolidation has taken place, but the ownership still remains fragmented, laying the ground for a competitive market structure.

Most of the approximately 8 TWh of generation in Northern Ireland is supplied by the vertically integrated Northern Ireland Electricity plc. from its three principal generation plants.

Figure **17**

Market Shares of UK Generation Companies, end-May 2005

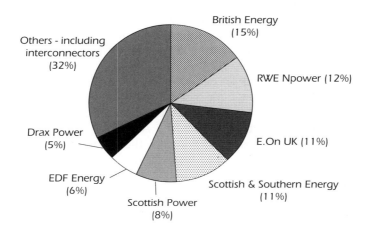

Source: The Department of Trade and Industry.

TRANSMISSION AND DISTRIBUTION NETWORKS

The National Grid owns the England and Wales transmission system and holds a licence for operating the Great Britain transmission system. The Scottish transmission system is owned by Scottish Power and Scottish and Southern Energy. Before the start of BETTA in 2005, the three British transmission companies were required to make annual SYSs that outlined their projections of supply, demand and transport needs; there is now a single GB-wide SYS which performs these roles.

The transmission grid in Great Britain is relatively strong and well developed. Broadly speaking, generation is concentrated in the north while demand is concentrated in the south. Hydropower resources in Scotland reinforce this picture and the large wind resources also concentrated in Scotland are likely to continue to pose a challenge for the system. Unsurprisingly, the most significant bottlenecks are between England and Scotland, and to some extent also further south on the north-south flow axis. Currently, there is a capability to transmit up to 2 000 MW from Scotland to England. According to the National Grid's SYS, from 2005 this capacity is already now short of the desired level and with projections for development in supply and demand, the desired transmission capacity will double within a few years.

Transmission charges are explicitly designed to reflect the long-run marginal cost of transporting one additional MW at any given node in the system. The charge is based on a sophisticated transmission flow modelling procedure, based on the forecasts established in the GB SYS. Since 2005/06 the Transmission Network Use of System (TNUoS) charges are calculated annually for 21 different generating zones and 14 demand zones covering all of Britain, although sub-annual TNUoS charges are also available for those generators that only wish to make use of the transmission network for shorter periods. Network users are also obliged to pay a transmission connection charge, bearing the direct costs of connecting to the transmission grid.

On the distribution side, the Utilities Act 2000 introduced distribution licences that have to be held by licensees who are legally separate from all supply activities. Licences for 14 distribution areas in Great Britain are currently held by seven different companies. Distribution and transmission networks have been subject to a system of price controls by the regulator since 1990. The fourth five-year distribution price control period began in April 2005 following a detailed review. The distribution grid price control had a stronger focus on investments compared to the past, allowing for a 48% increase in investments to accommodate higher expected shares of distributed generation and to uphold system security. The next GB-wide transmission price control period commences in April 2007.

Regulation of networks in Great Britain began with a focus on cost of operation. As a result, efficiency has improved and distribution tariffs have fallen by 50% in real terms since 1990 while transmission tariffs have fallen by 41%. A next phase of network regulation brought increasing focus on quality, rebalancing the incentives for investments in networks. A new phase has now begun where the network must be regulated to serve new needs and meet changing demand without losing either efficiency or quality. A new quality of service scheme was introduced into the network regulation in 2002 giving stronger emphasis on this aspect in the economic regulation. It includes a special incentive mechanism for companies to meet predefined quality of service targets measured in number of disruptions, severity of disruptions and customer treatment. During the first control period from 2003 to 2004, the average number of power cuts in distribution companies fell by 7% and the duration of power cuts fell by 6%.

RETAIL

Retail supply in the British electricity market is dominated by six large companies which supply 99% of consumers. Several of these companies have grown mainly through mergers and acquisitions while others have been successful with organic growth, primarily by marketing both gas and electricity. They each hold comparable shares in the retail market, with the smallest supplying 13% of customers and the largest supplying 21%. In September 2000, there were 10 larger companies supplying between 17% and 4% of consumers. These 10 companies also included independent retail companies only present on the retail side. In particular, since the introduction of NETA/BETTA, there has been a consolidation and vertical reintegration but the trend had already started in the late 1990s. All the current six large retailers have substantial generation assets ranging from a 3% share of installed capacity for BGT-Centrica, to 12% for npower. Vertically integrated companies with both retail and generation own some 50% of the total generating capacity.

Figure **18**

Retail Market Shares of Supply Companies in the UK, June 2005

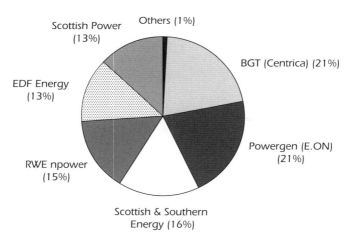

Source: Domestic Retail Market Report, June 2005, Ofgem.

Seven companies are registered in Northern Ireland to compete for supply of the approximately 1 000 customers large enough to be eligible to choose their supplier. One of these suppliers, Northern Ireland Electricity plc., supplies the remaining non-eligible customers at regulated prices.

Despite consolidation and reintegration, the supply market still seems to be competitive. All IEA member countries face challenges in organising proper retail competition that leads to substantial supplier switching by customers, particularly among small households. However, Great Britain has been successful in achieving this goal. Ofgem has monitored switching rates carefully since the opening of full retail competition for all consumers in May 1999. Already by the end of 2001, 38% of all consumers had switched supplier. By the end of 2003, 51% of all consumers had switched supplier at least once, of which some had switched back to the initial incumbent. Since 1999, the incumbent suppliers have seen a net loss of customers in their initial supply areas. By July 2005, 43% of all consumers had left their incumbent supplier. Approximately 350 000 consumers switched supplier each month from July 2003 to June 2005. Consumers have proven sensitive to price fluctuations. For example, anecdotal evidence suggests that one major electricity supplier lost 500 000 customers after it raised its prices. While many, if not most, retail supply companies compete through low prices, a number also offer premium product options such as longer-term contracts with fixed prices for one year or more.

One explanation for the successful switching rates and competition at the retail level is the establishment of the energy consumer watchdog, Energywatch. Energywatch was set up in November 2000 through the Utilities Act 2000 to protect and promote the interests of all electricity and gas consumers. Energywatch provides free, impartial information and takes up complaints by consumers. Energywatch has enabled transparent comparisons of offers and has dealt with some 70 000 complaints in 2004/05, down from some 110 000 in 2002/03.

ELECTRICITY PRICES

RETAIL PRICES

Electricity retail prices in the UK fell in real terms both for industry and households since the introduction of competition in 1991 up to 2003. The decrease in real prices for industry has been relatively smooth. A large part of the drop in household prices took place from 1996 until full retail competition in 1999. In 2004, prices increased slightly, a development which is likely to have intensified in 2005 as the result of increasing natural gas and coal prices and the introduction of the European CO_2 Emission Trading Scheme.

In 2004 retail prices in the UK, excluding taxes, were among the lowest third of IEA member countries for industry and among the mid-third for households. Electricity taxes for households were among the lowest in IEA member countries.

Figure **19**

Elecricity Prices in the UK and in Other Selected IEA Countries, 1980 to 2004

Industry Sector

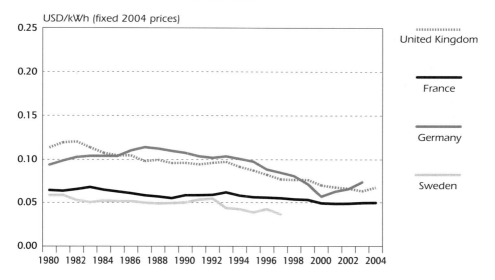

Household Sector

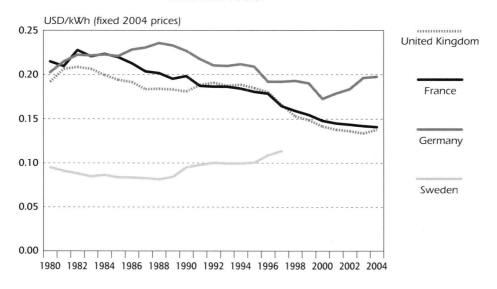

Source: *Energy Prices and Taxes*, IEA/OECD Paris, 2006.

Figure **20**

Electricity Prices in IEA Countries, 2005
Industry Sector

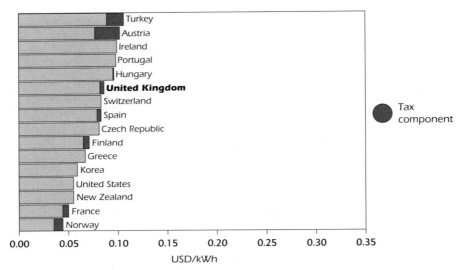

Note: Tax information not available for Korea. Price excluding tax for the United States. Data not available for Australia, Belgium, Canada, Denmark, Germany, Italy, Japan, Luxembourg, the Netherlands and Sweden.

Household Sector

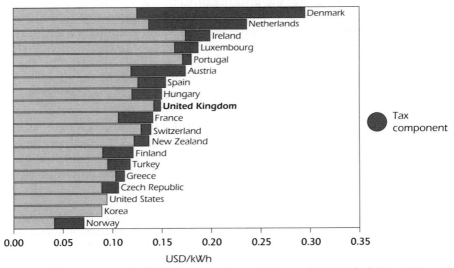

Note: Tax information not available for Korea. Price excluding tax for the United States. Data not available for Australia, Belgium, Canada, Germany, Italy, Japan and Sweden.

Source: *Energy Prices and Taxes*, IEA/OECD Paris, 2006.

WHOLESALE TRADE, BALANCING AND MARKET LIQUIDITY

Wholesale electricity trade in the electricity market of Great Britain is intended to unfold with a minimum of regulatory interference. With the introduction of NETA and now BETTA, the centralised Pool was abandoned for a far more decentralised trading system. Market players are free to trade as they see appropriate subject to financial incentives on parties to match their physical and contractual positions in "real time." This can take place through bilateral contracts that may be brokered in an "over the counter" (OTC) market or on an exchange. Trades are reported to the National Grid and are only binding from one hour before the moment of operation gate closure.

Overall the UK electricity market appears to be competitive and there are numerous market players ready to respond by investing in new generating capacity according to the needs of the market – e.g. in mid-2006 two new CCGTs, Langage (885 MW) and Marchwood (850 MW), were constructed. One of the key drivers is the retail market where very large numbers of consumers have shifted supplier since the opening of the market. There are still substantial price differentials among retail prices offering important gains to those who have still not switched, but all retail suppliers are faced with a real risk of losing substantial numbers of customers if prices are not competitive.

Since 2001 and 2002 when the diversity of companies in the sector saw a peak and traded liquidity also probably experienced a culmination, there has been a drive for vertical reintegration that would eventually constitute a real threat to competition if it were to continue. Liquidity in traded markets have also been falling since then, which is opposite to the development reported in other maturing electricity markets in Europe, North America and Australia. The drive for vertical reintegration was clear before the introduction of NETA, and has also been a trend in many other markets. However, there are certain features in the current trading arrangements that may contribute further to the drive for vertical reintegration and deteriorating liquidity compared to other IEA member countries. It could be considered if the merits these features are believed to bring outweigh the possible loss of liquidity.

The balancing mechanism is the trading arrangement that the National Grid uses to balance the system and ensure that all market participants are faced with financial incentives that contribute to overall system balance and efficiency. For the actual physical balancing, the National Grid acquires balancing resources from registered market participants. These are acquired through a mechanism where each supplier of balancing power is paid the price (in GBP/MWh) they successfully bid so as to unwind the excess demand/generation. This pricing principle also goes under the name of a discriminatory auction or pay-as-bid auction. In most other competitive electricity markets, the pricing principle also in the balancing markets is marginal pricing, where the highest market clearing bid sets the price for the entire market. The balancing mechanism has developed since its introduction and overall it serves its main objective well. Nevertheless, there are some features in the balancing mechanism and particularly the pay-as-bid principle that may have negative effects on liquidity.

The pay-as-bid principle resembles the bilateral trading approach, so in that sense it fits into the general logic of BETTA. It was also preferred to marginal pricing after careful consideration because it was regarded as more difficult for dominant market players to abuse and would thus lead to the most efficient and competitive prices. Much academic research explores the effectiveness of the pay-as-bid principle without giving clear conclusions. The National Grid has pointed out one less fortunate side-effect in a recent report, stating that, particularly in situations of tightness, it is likely that prices in the balancing mechanism are below marginal costs and that this could seriously undermine efficient market responses.

Another, perhaps more speculative, side-effect from the pay-as-bid principle may be that it is a barrier for certain smaller and independent market players. As far as the balancing mechanism constitutes a last resort, the prices are tightly related to the reference price for the entire market. All generators bidding into a pay-as-bid market are likely to try to predict the marginal cost of the marginal plant. They will bid as closely to this as possible if their own marginal costs are lower. In reality the pay-as-bid pricing may pose a greater risk for generators, compared to a marginal pricing system, particularly for certain technologies that must run. The risk of not being dispatched is a financial risk and they will have to bid into the market so that they can sell their production with great certainty. One way to avoid the risks of pay-as-bid is to link more closely with load through vertical integration of generation and supply. This may have added to the driving forces for further reintegration.

The independent National Grid subsidiary ELEXON manages the balancing mechanism by allocating the costs of balancing power to the beneficiaries. The costs are allocated through a dual pricing principle. Market players with imbalances that contribute to the total system imbalance are exposed to the imbalance price (System Buy Price or System Sell Price). Market players with an imbalance that helps to lower the total system imbalance are exposed to the "reverse" energy imbalance price derived from Market Index Data (MID). Since the introduction of this feature in 2003, the MID has been derived from traded products at the power exchange APX (formerly UKPX). This feature was introduced because it was considered a more accurate reflection of the actual costs of energy balancing on the part of the

Figure **21**

Daily Average Prices in the Balancing Mechanism, January 2002 to April 2006

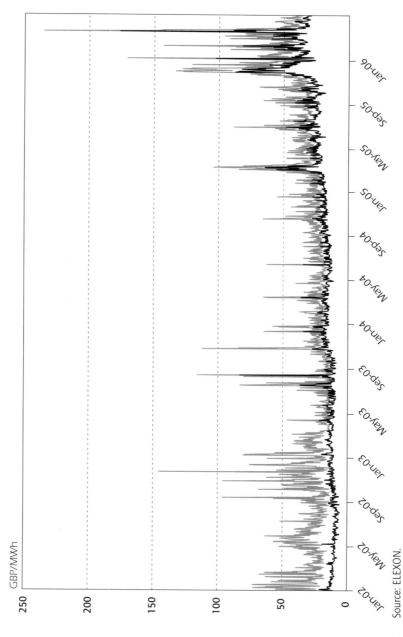

System buy price

System sell price

GBP/MWh

250

200

150

100

50

0

Jan-02
May-02
Sep-02
Jan-03
May-03
Sep-03
Jan-04
May-04
Sep-04
Jan-05
May-05
Sep-05
Jan-06

Source: ELEXON.

system operator, the National Grid, and is similar to other markets using a dual pricing mechanism for balancing, such as Sweden.

The prices for imbalances contributing to overall system imbalances are a weighted average of the prices paid to the suppliers of physical balancing services. It was intended that the discriminatory auction was to lead to bids close to marginal costs and hence weighted average prices close to marginal costs. Prices below marginal costs would undermine the incentives for new investments. The National Grid has argued in a consultation document that average prices in fact seemed to be below marginal costs, particularly in situations where supply and demand are tight. This could have distortionary effects on balancing incentives and incentives on investment, particularly in resources for peak load. On a proposition from the National Grid, Ofgem has consequently decided to change the composition of the imbalance price to one which is a weighted average of the last 100 MWh called on to balance the system. The price charged from market participants using the balancing mechanism thereby resembles the marginal price but the resources used for the balancing mechanism are still acquired on a pay-as-bid basis. The change has been controversial and has been contested by a variety of stakeholders. Concerns have been raised about the impact on *e.g.* market power, incentives and liquidity. Experience from other markets such as Norway and Australia show that real marginal pricing does not undermine the incentives for balancing. Particularly in Australia, marginal pricing in real time has been critical in attracting the necessary investments in peak load resources.

The aim of the balancing mechanism is to allocate the real costs of balancing the system according to the "polluter pay" principle. In effect, the dual pricing principle introduces an extra incentive for staying in balance. The dual pricing principle is also used in some other countries such as Sweden, and is the subject of on-going considerations in several markets. Dual pricing is intended to improve system security but it is not clear whether this is actually a measure that meets this objective efficiently. Market players would be expected to respond efficiently over time to prices that reflect nothing else but the real costs. One side-effect of the dual pricing principle is that imbalance charges can be reduced through aggregation. This does not diminish overall system imbalances but creates an artificial extra incentive for being a large market player, possibly thereby putting further pressure on liquidity.

The balancing mechanism determines balancing prices for the entire Great Britain market area. If there are internal bottlenecks in the transmission system, these are managed by acquiring balancing resources from the balancing mechanism. In 2006, the National Grid expects to spend GBP 42 million on managing congestions in the interconnection between England and Scotland. These expenditures are socialised across all users of the grid, and these costs are real and the result of the geographical distribution of generating, load and transmission capacity. There is no locational (nodal or zonal) price settlement so market players do not have transparent information enabling them to respond actively and efficiently to transmission constraints. Even if incentives for market players are blurred, Ofgem has introduced a very innovative and effective regulatory instrument that gives incentives to the National Grid to minimise congestion costs and maximise available transmission capacity. The lack of dynamic locational signals in the traded market is also somewhat compensated by the presence of locational network tariffs.

Only some 5% of the total Great Britain electricity demand is traded in the balancing mechanism. It was the intention that exchanges and over-the-counter (OTC) trade would develop from pressure from market participants. This would create liquidity in forward markets some years, months and weeks ahead of the moment of operation. A spot market for day-ahead and intra-day trade was also expected to develop. Dutch-based APX today owns the only exchange which offers spot trade. There are also other exchanges and brokers that offer spot trade and contracts with longer durations. According to the European Commission, sector inquiry exchange and OTC spot trade corresponded to almost 11% of total consumption from June 2004 to May 2005. Contracts with longer durations were brokered OTC in volumes corresponding to 146% of total consumption during the same period. This is not a sufficient level to qualify as a liquid market where market players can always expect to be able to manage the basic risks from fulfilling supply and demand obligations. There are reports of decreasing trading volumes in the UK market and significantly increasing volumes in several other markets such as the Nordic, German, Australian and US markets.

The relatively low, and possibly deteriorating, level of liquidity in the traded market may be a reason for concern, particularly considering the apparent pressure to vertically reintegrate retail and generation. If lack of small independent market players in Great Britain results from unnecessary barriers, there may be room for changes. Locational pricing, *e.g.* by introducing several or at least two zones, has been an important source of liquidity in the reference spot market in several other IEA member countries. One possibility to revitalise transparent trade is to use the French interconnector to take part in the French-Belgian-Dutch co-operation to establish implicit auctions across these countries. The merits and drawbacks of dual pricing, the pay-as-bid principle, and locational pricing within markets are discussed in several IEA member countries and there may be relevant lessons to be learnt from other markets, particularly relating to the impact these features have on liquidity.

CRITIQUE

In 1990/91, the UK was the first IEA member country to embark on a liberalisation process. This process has achieved remarkable results and offers important lessons for many other countries. The electricity sector has been fundamentally transformed under the increased pressure of competition. The technology and fuel mix now have a far higher share of gas-fired generation – though still relatively diverse – with improved efficiency and high levels of reliability. Consumers have a real choice of retailer and they have taken advantage of this choice to a greater extent than in almost all other IEA member countries. The establishment of the innovative consumer protection body, Energywatch, has played an important role to this end. The threat of losing customers puts ongoing effective competitive pressure on many parts of the electricity value chain.

The rapid and pronounced transformation of the generation portfolio through the 1990s under pressure from competition and as a response to the availability of abundant domestic gas and improved CCGT technology led to a substantial new generating capacity build. Reserve margins in terms of installed capacity to meet peak demand are still high even if relatively little new generating capacity has been added in recent years. But an array of challenges lies ahead and much clarity is necessary as soon as possible if market players are to respond to these challenges in an efficient way. With the new EU Large Combustion Plant Directive limiting the operation of older, large coal-fired power stations and with the decommissioning of ageing nuclear power plants, significant shares of installed capacity will be lost as from 2010 through the following 10-15 years. At the same time, the government is one of the strongest proponents for the need to urgently address the impact of GHG emissions.

The current market structure appears to be sufficiently competitive. While wholesale and retail prices have risen in the last several years, there is little evidence (and few accusations) that this results from collusion. Although proof of such market power abuse can be extremely difficult to detect, rising gas and coal prices, along with the introduction of the EU-ETS, are the most likely causes of electricity price increases. However, the vertical integration that has taken place during the last five years and the reduction of market players, particularly on the retail side, makes ongoing market monitoring to ensure continued competition even more important in the future. Consolidation and other changes in the structure of the industry can be driven by apparent synergies and economies of scale and scope. However, other drivers may also be at play, most worryingly a desire by large players to be able to influence prices.

Liquidity has decreased markedly during the same period making it even more difficult for smaller independent market operators to take part in the market. Volumes of wholesale trade in several other IEA member countries have recently increased substantially, which is an even stronger reason for concern over the low and decreasing level of traded volumes in the GB market. This development calls for close monitoring and analysis, particularly where this was triggered by the organisation and regulation of the market. The structure of the industry today ensures substantial competitive pressure among the several generators and the six large retailers, but a continued drive for vertical integration and perhaps further consolidation can pose a serious threat on competition in the future.

Transparency and effective dissemination of market information becomes particularly important with growing horizontal and vertical consolidation. A continuous flow of information about supply and demand fundamentals, including appropriate real-time information on generation plants, is crucial for an effective market. DTI, Ofgem and National Grid provide an impressive amount of information to the public domain and it is important that this flow of information is assessed and adapted to the needs of the market. Currently this information does not include immediate changes in the status of generation plants. This can potentially constitute an important source for insider information. Models for dissemination of information to avoid opportunities for insider trading are currently developing in several IEA member countries, including EU member states, and Ofgem is encouraged to follow this development proactively.

Most of the market design features in the original mandatory Pool were changed with the introduction of NETA in 2001 and extended to Scotland through BETTA in 2005. During the first 10 years of operation with the Pool, several weaknesses emerged and the introduction of NETA was a timely reaction to this need for adaptation. NETA/BETTA has now operated for some five years and several apparent weaknesses in the new trading arrangements have emerged, and some intended developments have not materialised.

One of the distinct features of the new trading arrangements was their very light-handed regulation in terms of formal trading and pricing principles, effectively abolishing the mandatory Pool. It was expected that various liquid forward markets would develop through commercial exchanges, including a day-ahead spot market. This has not materialised. The current level of forward trading is not very liquid and transparent, and a spot market setting a strong reference price has not emerged. Another distinct feature is the pay-as-bid pricing principle in the balancing mechanism which is contrary to pricing principles employed in most competitive electricity markets. Pay-as-bid was partly chosen because it was intended to reduce market power abuse. It is unclear whether this objective is met more effectively than with marginal pricing. On the other hand, there are a number of possible negative effects, such as prices below marginal costs, particularly in situations of stress, which does not encourage efficient market response. The pay-as-bid feature, in combination with the fact that the balancing settlement includes an additional financial incentive on top of the real costs of balancing that can be reduced through aggregation of load, could also act to limit liquidity by giving stronger incentives for mergers and vertical integration. Finally, the BETTA is also lacking transparent locational pricing as transmission congestion is managed through redispatch. The increased transparency from nodal or zonal prices has helped boost liquidity in many other voluntary spot markets in other countries. The government should consider re-evaluating the merits and drawbacks of pay-as-bid pricing, dual pricing charges in the balancing mechanism and the lack of locational signals in electricity trading in order to adjust the market design to the benefit of market liquidity and efficiency.

The UK is a role model among IEA member countries when it comes to regulation of networks. The regulator, Ofgem, has continued to adjust and adapt regulation to push for efficiency without jeopardising reliability. Ofgem's groundbreaking work in this area offers many lessons for other countries. Many innovative incentive-based measures have been implemented with great success. Being a leader in the ongoing efforts to create a regulatory framework that allows real market incentives also creates the challenge of carefully monitoring the results in terms of efficiency, reliability and administrative burden.

A new phase has now started where the network will have to focus increasingly on new needs and changing demand without losing efficiency or quality. The Renewables Obligation has already brought new distributed and intermittent renewable power in the form of wind, and much more is expected in the coming years. At the other end of the scale, nuclear power is receiving more attention with possible future connections of very large nuclear units to the grid. It is a challenge to regulate the development of the grid in a way that accommodates these needs in a balanced way that also offers a level playing field for all technologies. Support for specific technologies by socialising network costs does not lead to a level playing field and undermines the transparency of various policy measures. Therefore, it is now particularly important that Ofgem continues to take a leading role in developing innovative network regulation that assures a level playing field for all technologies.

RECOMMENDATIONS

The government of the United Kingdom should:

▶ *Closely monitor the development of vertical integration of retail and generation in relation to the impact on competition and liquidity.*

▶ *Continue efforts to make fundamental information and analysis on supply and demand readily available to the market in order to ensure the investment environment is as transparent as possible.*

▶ *Consider ways to improve the framework for enhanced electricity market liquidity and enable the establishment of a strong reference price, e.g. through:*

- *Working with the regulator Ofgem to adjust the pricing principles in the balancing mechanism with particular attention paid to the impact on the ability for new independent market players to take positions in the market.*

- *Extending the locational signals, currently embedded in the network charges for generation, to traded electricity in the balancing mechanism in order to enhance transparency in the real-time wholesale pricing of electricity.*

COAL

In 2004, coal accounted for 37.5 Mtoe of primary energy supply, or 16.0% of national total primary energy supply (TPES). Coal's contribution to UK TPES has fallen by more than half since 1973 when it accounted for 34.6% of all energy supply. Coal's decreasing importance in the UK energy mix resulted from the unwinding of subsidies to domestic coal production in the late 1980s and the emergence of inexpensive natural gas from the UK Continental Shelf (UKCS) in the North Sea.

The large majority of coal in the UK is used for electricity and heat generation. In 2004, electricity and heat generation accounted for 91% of all coal supply. This percentage has been steadily rising over the years as coal's application as an end-use fuel diminishes. In 1973, coal's use for electricity and heat generation accounted for 68% of coal supply. At the same time, the percentage of UK power generation coming from coal has substantially decreased. In 1973, coal accounted for 62% of all UK generation, while by 2004 it had dropped to only 34% of total generation. Coal consumption as an end-use fuel is split between the industrial and the residential sectors. In 2004, 64% of all coal end-use took place in industry. This figure has fluctuated between 50% and 65% over the last ten years.

Domestic coal production has been in decline for many years. The highest UK coal production came in 1913 when production was approximately 12 times greater than it is today. Since the founding of the IEA in 1973, coal production has fallen by 80%. In 2005, domestic production was 14.9 Mtoe, approximately 40% of that year's supply of coal for the UK. The remainder is made up of imports from the international market. In 2005, major exporting countries to the UK were South Africa, Russia and Australia.

In 2005, total domestic coal production was 20.0 million tonnes, with 9.6 million tonnes from deep mines and 10.4 million tonnes from opencast sites. In December 2005, there were eight major deep mines in production and four smaller mines. There were 34 opencast sites in production and five sites developing. Industry is in private ownership. Recent problems have forced the closure of two deep mines and the mothballing of a third.

Since the December 1994 sale of the state-owned British Coal Corporation, all coal mining in Great Britain has been carried out by the private sector. The State, in the form of the Coal Authority (a non-departmental public body funded by DTI), remains the freehold owner of unworked coal reserves. Mining operators currently exploit the resource under leases and licences granted either by the

Secretary of State of Trade and Industry or the Authority under the Coal Industry Act 1994. No royalty is payable in respect to licences issued at privatisation as the value of the coal was reflected in the sales proceeds received at that time. For the licences subsequently granted by the Coal Authority, production-related rent is levied on tonnage output. Although the rate varies between sites it has, since 2003, been subject to an upper limit of 10 pence per tonne. Total production-related receipts in 2004/05 were GBP 650 000.

A new state aid scheme, Coal Investment Aid (CIA) was introduced in 2003. The CIA makes up to GBP 60 million available to maintain access to viable reserves at mines which were in operation during July-December 2002. Successful applicants receive up to 30% funding for projects which maintain access to coal reserves and safeguard or create employment. The available funding has all been allocated and is expected to be drawn down by end-2006. CIA is paid to reimburse eligible investment costs as they are incurred and defrayed.

OFFSHORE OIL AND GAS PRODUCTION AND INFRASTRUCTURE

PRODUCTION

In 2004, the UK produced 99.6 Mtoe of oil and 86.4 Mtoe of natural gas. Together with coal, this production made the UK the fifth-largest fossil fuel producer in the IEA (behind the United States, Canada, Australia and Norway). It was the IEA's third-largest gas producer and the fourth-largest oil producer.

UK domestic oil production peaked in 1999 and gas production peaked in 2000. The large majority of the fields are mature and declining. In general, the country has already produced about 70% of its total possible oil reserves and 65% of its total possible gas reserves. Some recent finds, primarily the Buzzard field, are expected to increase oil production in 2007, but the long-term trend for both oil and gas is for continuing declines. Figure 22 shows historical and projected production.

A survey covering operators' intentions to invest in the UK Continental Shelf (UKCS) oil and gas production was conducted in the autumn of 2005, a time when oil and gas prices were very high by historical standards. The survey indicates that total development capital expenditure is at the highest level since 1998 (GBP 4.4 billion in 2005 and around GBP 4.8 billion in 2006). Post-2006, the development capital expenditure will gradually fall. Such a decline is expected since companies have not formulated their investment plans for these years.

Figure 22

Historical and Projected Domestic UK Oil and Gas Production

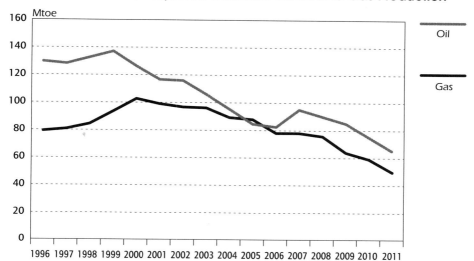

Note: Projections represent average of range provided by DTI. In general, the upper and lower limits of this range are about 10% above and below the average cited.

Source: Department of Trade and Industry.

Table 19

Estimates of Remaining UK Oil and Gas Reserves

(as of 31 December 2004)

OIL, million tonnes

	Proven	Probable	Prov. & Prob.	Possible	Maximum
Remaining reserve estimates	533	213	747	393	1 139
Cumulative production (year-end 2005)	3 089				
Oil production, 2005	84				
Remaining production years at 2005 level[1]	5.3	n/a	7.9	n/a	12.6

NATURAL GAS, billion cubic metres[2]

	Proven	Probable	Prov. & Prob.	Possible	Maximum
Remaining reserve estimates	531	296	826	343	1 169
Cumulative production (year-end 2005)	1 921				
Oil production, 2005	93				
Remaining production years at 2005 level[2]	4.7	n/a	7.9	n/a	11.6

1. This assumes one year of production (2005) from reserve estimates cited. It also includes 2006 as a year of remaining production.

2. Includes dry gas, gas from condensate fields and associated gas.

Source: DTI Oil and Gas Statistics.

PRODUCTION INFRASTRUCTURE

The production infrastructure in the UKCS is some of the most advanced and extensive in the world. Data on the fields and related platforms and pipelines are given below.[24]

Offshore oil and gas fields	
Number of oil and gas fields approved in 1975 and before	19
Number of oilfields approved since 1976	159
Number of condensate fields approved since 1976	29
Number of gas fields approved since 1976	122
Total offshore fields approved	329
Number of operators granted field licences	approximately 35
Offshore oil and gas platforms	
Number of oil platforms	85
Number of floating installations	18
Total number of oil installations	103
Number of gas platforms	169
Total number of oil and gas installations	272
Offshore oil and gas pipelines	
Number of associated gas pipelines	48
Total length of associated gas pipelines (km)	3 397
Number of condensate pipelines	14
Total length of condensate pipelines (km)	425
Number of crude oil pipelines	128
Total length of crude oil pipelines (km)	3 458
Number of natural gas pipelines	130
Total length of natural gas pipelines (km)	4 891
Number of other pipelines	9
Length of other pipelines (km)	144
Total number of pipelines	329
Total length of pipeline network (km)	12 315

PRODUCTION POLICIES, LICENSING AND FISCAL REGIME

Government policy strives to maximise economic production from domestic reserves as long as possible. Given the maturity of the UKCS, the addition of two new types of licence has been central to maintaining interest and

---

24. All production infrastructure data from DTI Oil and Gas Statistics.

investment. These are: *i)* the "promote" licence, at a tenth of the cost of a traditional licence for the first two years, to attract new smaller investors, and *ii)* the "frontier" licence, to ensure the maximum opportunity for appraisal of prospects west of Shetland. The frontier licences have been available in both the 22nd (2004) and 23rd (2005) rounds. This new type of licence allows companies to take larger areas in the first instance. Licence rentals in the first two years are low, allowing companies to do initial screenings/evaluations over larger areas with greater materiality, but 75% of the original area has to be given up after two years, in addition to the familiar 50% relinquishment of area "acreage" at the end of the exploration phase. It offers six years in which to complete the exploration-phase work programme, two years longer than the more traditional production licence. Thirteen frontier licences have been issued so far, seven in 2004 and six in 2005, and this type of licence will now feature as a regular element in the annual offshore licensing rounds.

In addition, the "fallow" exercise, introduced in 2001, continues to ensure that companies are unable to hold onto licensed acreage where there is little or no activity, thereby maximising scope for exploration and development.

The fiscal regime which currently applies to oil and gas exploration and extraction from the UK and the UKCS (the North Sea fiscal regime) consists of three elements:

- **Ring fence corporation tax:** With some important modifications (*e.g.* relating to capital allowances and losses), this is the standard corporation tax applicable to all companies, with the addition of a "ring fence" and 100% first-year allowances for almost all capital expenditure. The ring fence prevents taxable profits from oil and gas extraction in the UK and UKCS being reduced by losses from other activities or by excessive interest payments by treating ring fenced activities as a separate trade. The current rate of corporation tax is 30%.

- **Supplementary charge:** This is an additional charge of 20% on a company's ring fence profits excluding finance costs. This charge was introduced at 10% in April 2002 and was accompanied by the introduction of 100% first-year relief against both the supplementary charge and the ring fence corporation tax for virtually all North Sea capital expenditure. In addition, the fiscal regime was simplified with the abolition with effect from 1 January 2003 of the royalty that applied to production from older fields. In the pre-Budget Statement of 2005, the supplementary charge was increased to 20%.

- **Petroleum revenue tax (PRT):** This is a special tax on oil and gas production from the UK and UKCS. It is a field-based tax charged on profits arising from individual oilfields. The current rate of PRT is 50%. PRT was abolished for all fields given development consent on or after 16 March 1993. PRT is deductible as an expense against corporation tax and the supplementary charge. The marginal tax rate on new fields is 50% while the marginal tax rate on fields paying PRT is 75%.

The government also announced in December 2005 that it was opening discussions with the oil and gas industry to tackle wider structural issues which affect the stability of the North Sea fiscal regime. The increase in the rate of the supplementary charge was in response to the sustained increase in oil prices and an upward shift in expectations of oil prices in the medium term. It ensures that the regime continues to strike the right balance between oil producers and consumers by promoting investment and ensuring fairness for taxpayers; oil companies should receive a fair post-tax return for their risk and investment in the North Sea and the UK needs to get a fair share of the revenues derived from a national resource.

The DTI is now committed to annual licensing rounds to allow industry to plan its likely investment strategies more effectively. Strategic environmental assessments have been carried out for a large proportion of the UK territory to allow DTI to make as much acreage as possible available for exploration and development via successive licensing rounds.

Through its UK offshore oil and gas promotional work, the DTI is also continuing to highlight and promote exploration potential west of Shetland, both via presentations to industry and papers made available by the Energy Resources and Development Unit. A recent substantial discovery in 2004 (Rosebank/Lochnagar) has also generated more interest in the area. However, there is currently considerable industry concern about the low overall availability of drilling rigs, which could potentially hold up exploration both west of Shetland and in the North Sea.

On the commercial side, DTI has been working with industry to ensure that the North Sea commercial climate is attractive to a range of players large and small. Industry has agreed an Infrastructure Code of Practice to help ensure that third-party access to infrastructure can be achieved on fair and reasonable terms. If a stalemate situation should arise, the government has the right to intervene and set a tariff. Industry has also signed up to a Commercial Code of Practice to promote non-blocking commercial behaviours on the UKCS.

Alongside standardised agreements such as the "Master Deed" which is now used by a number of licensees for standard North Sea asset transactions, industry has also signed up to a Commercial Code of Practice. This ensures that North Sea deals are being carried out as smoothly and effectively as possible, with the opportunity to spread "best practice".

Reaction to these changes has been positive. In 2005, the highest number of licences was awarded in UK North Sea history: 152 licences in total, covering 266 blocks. The spread of awards covered 70 Traditional, 76 Promote and six Frontier licences, with very strong competition for some blocks. Seventeen firm drilling commitments were made.

DOWNSTREAM OIL

SUPPLY AND DEMAND

In 2004, oil was the UK's second-most widely used fuel (after natural gas), accounting for 35.8% of national TPES. Oil's share of TPES for all IEA countries combined was 40.6% in 2004. The government forecasts that primary oil supply to the UK will grow in absolute terms from 83.7 Mtoe in 2004 to 86.9 Mtoe in 2010 and 95.9 Mtoe in 2030. Its share of TPES is projected to rise to 38.9% by 2020.

Oil's share of electricity generation has fallen since the 1970s. In 1973, oil accounted for 25.6% of total generation but fell to 10.9% in 1990 and 1.2% in 2004. The transport sector is currently by far the greatest final consumer of oil and oil products. In 2004, transport accounted for 70.1% of oil TFC with road transport accounting for 74% of this amount. Petroleum for non-energy use accounted for 13.9% of oil final consumption, followed by industry (10.2%), residences (3.8%) and commercial, agriculture and the public sector (2.0% combined). From 1994 to 2004, oil TFC increased annually by 0.5%. Over the same period, oil use in industry grew the most rapidly (1.6% per annum), followed by transport (1.3%) and residences (0.3%).

Figure **23**

Final Consumption of Oil by Sector, 1973 to 2020

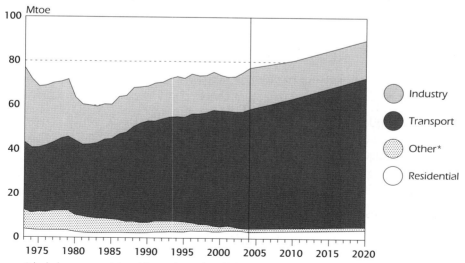

* includes commercial, public service and agricultural sectors.

Sources: *Energy Balances of OECD Countries*, IEA/OECD Paris, 2006 and country submission.

RETAIL AND REFINING INDUSTRY STRUCTURE

The UK operates an open market with no government ownership within the downstream sector. The table below shows market share by forecourt brand for road fuels (petrol and diesel) for the year to July 2006.

_____ Table **20**
Market Share by Brand, Year to July 2006

BP	16.1%
Tesco	12.8%
Esso	11.5%
Shell	11.5%
Total	8.6%
Morrisons	8.2%
Texaco	8.0%
Sainsburys	7.8%
Others	15.5%

Source: Catalyst.

The UK has a refining capacity of a little over 90 million tonnes (Mt) per year, compared to a demand of about 78 Mt. Thus, the UK is an overall net exporter of oil products, although a significant net importer of aviation fuel. Environmental pressures have led to both cleaner fuel regulations and a demand change in surface transport fuels (dieselisation). This has left the UK being a marginal importer of diesel but with a significant surplus (5 Mt) of gasoline to export.

OIL PRODUCT PRICES AND TAXATION

The UK operates an open market where the market sets the price of petroleum products at the forecourt. Government influences prices solely through taxation. In general, UK ex tax prices for motor fuels are at or below the OECD average while the taxes are among the highest in the OECD. In the fourth quarter 2005, the UK ex tax price for petrol was 7% below the IEA average, but the taxes paid were 37% above the average and the final price to consumers almost 20% above the average.[25] The UK has the fifth-highest retail prices for petrol in the IEA. For diesel fuel, the UK ex tax prices are 6% below the IEA average,[26] while diesel taxes are 80% above the IEA average and the final retail price is 36% above the average. The UK had the highest price for diesel fuel in the IEA, more than 8% above the next countries (Norway and Sweden).

---

25. Data not available for Greece.
26. Data from Greece and Canada not available.

Figure 24

OECD Unleaded Gasoline Prices and Taxes, Second Quarter 2006

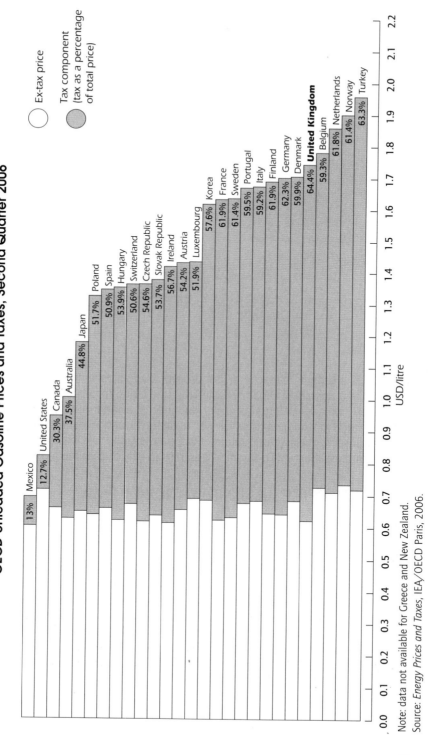

○ Ex-tax price

◐ Tax component
(tax as a percentage
of total price)

Mexico 13%
United States 12.7%
Canada 30.3%
Australia 37.5%
Japan 44.8%
Poland 51.7%
Spain 50.9%
Hungary 53.9%
Switzerland 50.6%
Czech Republic 54.6%
Slovak Republic 53.7%
Ireland 56.7%
Austria 54.2%
Luxembourg 51.9%
Korea 57.6%
France 61.9%
Sweden 61.4%
Portugal 59.5%
Italy 59.2%
Finland 61.9%
Germany 62.3%
Denmark 59.9%
United Kingdom 64.4%
Belgium 59.3%
Netherlands 61.8%
Norway 61.4%
Turkey 63.3%

USD/litre

0.0 0.1 0.2 0.3 0.4 0.5 0.6 0.7 0.8 0.9 1.0 1.1 1.2 1.3 1.4 1.5 1.6 1.7 1.8 1.9 2.0 2.1 2.2

Note: data not available for Greece and New Zealand.

Source: *Energy Prices and Taxes*, IEA/OECD Paris, 2006.

— Figure **25** —

OECD Automotive Diesel Prices and Taxes, Second Quarter 2006

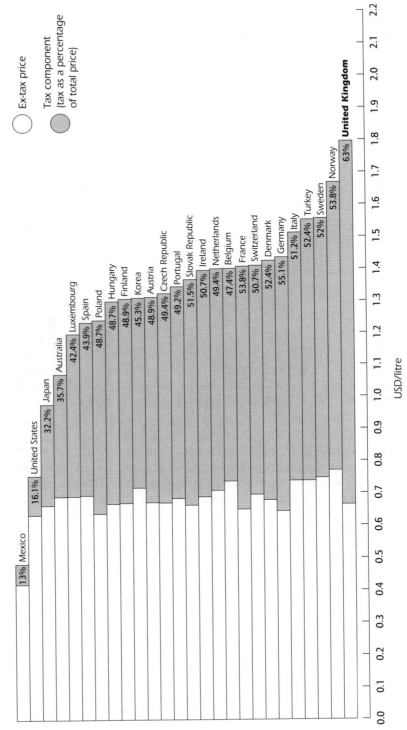

○ Ex-tax price

◐ Tax component (tax as a percentage of total price)

Mexico 13%
United States 16.1%
Japan 32.2%
Australia 35.7%
Luxembourg 42.4%
Spain 43.9%
Poland 48.7%
Hungary 48.7%
Finland 48.9%
Korea 45.3%
Austria 48.9%
Czech Republic 49.4%
Portugal 49.2%
Slovak Republic 51.5%
Ireland 50.7%
Netherlands 49.4%
Belgium 47.4%
France 53.8%
Switzerland 50.7%
Denmark 52.4%
Germany 55.1%
Italy 51.2%
Turkey 52.4%
Sweden 52%
Norway 53.8%
United Kingdom 63%

USD/litre

Note: data not available for Canada, Greece and New Zealand.
Source: *Energy Prices and Taxes*, IEA/OECD Paris, 2006.

EMERGENCY PREPAREDNESS

The Energy Act 1976 provides the legislative basis for action by the UK to implement its obligations under the IEA's International Energy Program (IEP) or, in the event of national emergency, to control the production, supply, acquisition and use of oil and oil products. Consistent with the IEA Governing Board decision of 1995, if an oil crisis arises, the UK would expect stockdraw, demand restraint and complementary measures to form the first stage of any international action. Although the UK is a net exporter of oil and therefore not obliged to hold stocks under the IEP, it is obliged to hold stocks equivalent to 67.5 days of the previous year's consumption in accordance with EU directives, under which it is given a 25% derogation to account for its net exporter status. These stocks are commingled with company operating stocks.

Events relevant to the UK's emergency response capability, including the 2000 fuel protests, post-11 September 2001, the war in Iraq and hurricane Katrina. Following the fuel protests, a task force was established involving ministers, the oil industry, the police, the trade unions and road haulers to develop a series of practical arrangements involving all the key parties aimed at maintaining the continuity of domestic oil supply. This work resulted in a Memorandum of Understanding (MoU) of 2000, signed by a number of parties, including the oil companies, police and trade unions. Domestic and international plans have continued to be reviewed and revised since then.

Considerable changes have also occurred in the oil market, including a decline in production, a levelling of domestic demand and restructuring of oil company operations. A number of factors make it problematic for the current stockholding system to meet the existing EU obligations, especially in Category 2 (middle distillates). These include: the growing market share of companies with lower obligations, such as hypermarkets; the sale by some refiners of parts of their retail networks (thus excluded from obligations); and the general falling level of stocks held in refineries (with just-in-time, etc.) which can be used to back up the obligation stocks.

The decline in production will eventually lead to the end of the EU stockholding derogation for domestic production. The government expects the country will continue to have the maximum EU derogation of 25% until production falls below 25% of consumption. On current trends, this will occur between 2010 and 2015. It will then decline gradually, ending completely when UK production halts. The UK obligation will, therefore, gradually increase by one-third to 90 days in the medium term.

The UK will also need to comply with the IEA stockholding obligations once it ceases to be a net exporter of oil. The DTI anticipates that the UK's IEA stockholding obligation is likely to remain lower than the EU obligation for most of the period before UK exports fall to zero. However, by the end of the period, the IEA obligation will involve a further increase of about 10% for unavailable stocks (*i.e.* tank bottoms) which are excluded from IEA emergency reserve calculations.

The government acknowledges that the decline in production will increase its EU oil stockholding obligations and that, because of this and other factors, it needs to review its stockholding system. Under the direction of DTI, in 2003/04 the UK undertook a formal consultation exercise of their stockholding arrangements with the industry. The government proposed that, in order to address the difficulty in meeting the Category 2 obligation, it would move the basis for calculating the obligations from sales into final consumption to products entering the UK from refineries or as imports. It also said that it would maintain its longstanding policy position that the most efficient, economical and transparent stockholding policy for the UK is to continue with compulsory stockholding for oil companies, rather than through a government-owned stock system or agency system.

IEA STOCK RELEASE OF SEPTEMBER 2005

As part of the collective action, the UK agreed to contribute some 2.2 million barrels over September 2005 as its share of the IEA collection response to hurricanes Katrina and Rita, equating to some 280 thousand tonnes of oil products. The UK implemented the contribution by reducing the number of days of compulsory stocks for industry. For non-refiners, the direction was prescriptive and reduced the Category 1 (gasoline) obligation by five days. Refiners were given more flexibility by reducing their overall obligation by two days (varying between 5 days for Category 1 or two-and-a-half days for the middle distillate Category 2). The UK released some 600 thousand barrels of crude oil stocks, 1.2 million barrels of gasoline stocks and 450 million barrels of middle distillates.

DOWNSTREAM NATURAL GAS

NATURAL GAS SUPPLY AND DEMAND

In 2004, natural gas accounted for 87.4 Mtoe of primary energy supply, or 37.4% of the total for all fuels. In the past five years, the gas supply share has stayed relatively stable – in 2000, the share was 37.5% – but has increased substantially over the long term. In 1973, gas accounted for just 11.4% of UK TPES, while by 1991 it had risen to 23.2%. The discovery and production from the North Sea, as well as the decrease in coal subsidies and domestic mining, were the major drivers of increased gas supply. The government projects that gas's share of TPES will rise, but only slightly, reaching 39.4% in 2020.

A substantial percentage of UK gas supply is used to generate electricity and heat. In 2004, gas-fired power plants generated 41% of all UK electricity. This figure has seen tremendous growth in the past 15 years with the introduction of North Sea gas and CCGT plants which benefited from the introduction of competition and technology development. In 1990, gas accounted for just 1.6% of the UK electricity generation. One UK government report projects that gas will increase its share of the electricity market to 60.6% by 2020.

In 2004, gas final consumption accounted for 59% of supply. This demand is dominated by the residential and industrial sectors. In 2004, residences accounted for 60% of gas final demand while industry accounted for 22%. Other gas demand comes from the commercial and public sectors.

IMPORTS, EXPORTS AND PROJECTED INFRASTRUCTURE NEEDS

Through the 1990s, both UK domestic production and UK demand for gas grew rapidly. From 1990 to 2000, production more than doubled, reaching its peak in 2000 at 97.5 Mtoe. To give an idea of the scale of this added production, the amount by which the UK increased its gas production in just those ten years was greater than the 2005 TPES for Austria and Portugal combined. Since 2000, however, production has gone down. Already in 2004, production had dropped to 86.4 Mtoe, or more than 10% below the 2000 peak. In 2004, the UK became a net importer of gas for the first time since 1996. All forecasts expect continuing production declines, increasing demand and thus growing levels of net imports. Figure 26 shows historical production, imports and exports.

In 2004, gas imports came from both Norway and Belgium.[27] Norwegian gas comes directly from the Norwegian North Sea gas fields via subsea pipes. While Norway is a simple gas exporter to the UK, Belgium both imports and exports gas depending on the relative market conditions in the UK and on the continent. Gas is traded with Belgium via the interconnector connecting Zeebrugge in Belgium with Bacton in the UK. Despite the UK's generally growing gas import dependence, it remains a strong net gas exporter to the continent. In 2004, the UK exported 6 565 mcm to Belgium and imported just 3 428 mcm, for a net export for the year of 3 137. In the same year, there were 8 678 mcm of imports from Norway (with no exports) and 3 557 mcm of exports to the Republic of Ireland (with no imports).

---

27. Belgium has no domestic production. Gas imported to the UK via the subsea pipeline to Belgium is either Dutch or comes from farther East.

Figure 26

Historical UK Gas Production, Imports and Exports, 1973 to 2004

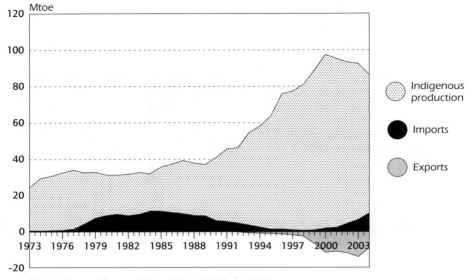

Source: *Energy Prices and Taxes*, IEA/OECD Paris, 2006.

The growing levels of imports to meet projected UK demand cannot be met with the existing import infrastructure. The National Grid, the UK owner and operator of the high-pressure gas pipelines and the high-voltage electricity network among other activities, produces a report every year which projects expected supply and demand ten years into the future. The latest such report, *Gas Transportation Ten Year Statement*, was released in December 2005. In this report, the National Grid forecasts likely domestic demand, domestic production and imports from existing, under construction and planned pipelines, and LNG import facilities. It projects that the country's import dependence will grow to 52% by 2011/12 and to 81% by 2014/15.

Figure 27 shows the National Grid's expected demand forecasts as well as the various sources of supply that will come to meet it. Please note that the figures in the graph correspond to a 75% capacity factor for all import projects. All existing projects and projects under construction as of December 2005 are included in the categories Norwegian imports, Continental imports and Other imports. Proposed projects are included in Other imports.

The growing import dependence will require new import capacity. Table 21 below shows the projects that are planned and under construction.

Figure **27**

Forecast UK Demand and Domestic and Imported Supply

(assumed load factor of 75% for all import projects)

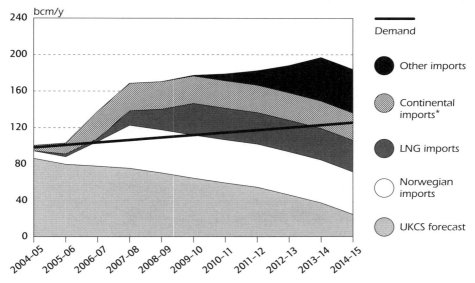

*Continental imports" refers to imports received via interconnectors to the European mainland.
Source: "Gas Transportation Ten Year Statement," National Grid; December 2005.

The development of gas storage projects in the UK has faced difficulties. Such difficulties relate primarily to obtaining the proper planning permissions and to confront related local opposition. In May 2006, the Trade and Industry Secretary issued a statement addressing the urgency of new gas infrastructure with specific focus on gas storage facilities. Citing the difficulties some companies have had in constructing such facilities, he announced three measures to assist them:

- Legislation will be established to allow innovative projects (*e.g.* gas storage in offshore salt caverns and LNG projects with offshore unloading) to go ahead.

- A review of onshore consents regimes aimed at simplifying and streamlining will be launched.

- Measures to improve public understanding of the need for new gas infrastructure will be taken.

ONSHORE PIPELINE NETWORK

The gas transportation system throughout Great Britain is operated by the National Grid and regulated by Ofgem. The high-pressure network consists of

_____ Table **21**

Gas Import Projects

Project	Developer	Location	Size (per annum)	Date	Status
Belgium Interconnector (IUK, Phase II)	IUK	Zeebrugge to Bacton	Additional 7 bcm	Dec 2006	Under construction
Langeled	Gassco	Sleipner to Easington	25 bcm	Majority ready by Q4 2006, rest 2007-08	Under construction
Dutch interconnector (BBL)	BBL	Balgzand to Bacton	16 bcm	2006-2007	Under construction
Tampen Link	Gassco	New link to existing LNG infrastructure	~10 bcm	2007-2008	Construction contract awarded
Isle of Grain LNG (Phase II)	National Grid	Isle of Grain	Additional 9 bcm	2008-2009	Construction contract awarded
Dragon LNG	Petroplus/BG /Petronas	Milford Haven	6 bcm	2007-2008	Under construction
South Hook LNG (Phase I)	Qatar Petroleum /ExxonMobil	Milford Haven	10.5 bcm	2007-2008	Under construction
South Hook LNG (Phase II)	Qatar Petroleum /ExxonMobil	Milford Haven	10.5 bcm	2008-2009	Construction contract awarded
Canvey LNG	Calor Gas, Centrica, Japan LNG	Canvey Island	5.4 bcm	2010	Initial development
Amlwch LNG	Canatxx	Isle of Anglesey	15 bcm	2010	Initial development
Other LNG	Numerous others	Numerous		2010+	Conceptual

Source: *Gas Transportation Ten Year Statement*, the National Grid, December 2005.

6 800 miles of pipelines, 25 compressor stations and seven coastal terminals: St Fergus (where the majority of UK production enters the system), Barrow, Teesside, Easington, Theddlethorpe, Bacton Interconnector and Isle of Grain (where the first phase of an LNG terminal was brought on line in July 2005.) Prices for use of the transmission system are fully regulated to allow the National Grid to earn a reasonable rate of return. The tariffs will be based on an "RPI-X" price control formula until March 2007 with a 6.25% allowed rate of return on

Table ㉒
Gas Storage Projects

Project	Developer	Location	Size (mcm)	Date	Status
Aldbrough	Statoil/SSE	Aldbrough	420	2007/08	Under construction
Holford Gas Storage	E-On	Byley	165	2008/09	Under development
Welton	Star Energy	Lincolnshire	435	2008/09	Planning permission pending
Albury (Phase I)	Star Energy	Surrey	160	2008/09	Initial stages
Albury (Phase II)	Star Energy	Surrey	~715	2010	Conceptual
Bletchingley	Star Energy	Surrey	~875	2009	Conceptual
Caythorpe	Warwick Energy	East Yorkshire	200	2007	Planning permission pending
Stublach	Ineos Enterprises	Cheshire	550	2009	Initial stages
Saltfleetby	Wingas	Lincolnshire	600+	2009	Initial stages
Portland	Egdon Resources	Isle of Portland	300+	2008	Initial stages
Fleetwood	Canatxx	Fleetwood	1 700	2009/10	Public enquiry under way

Source: *Gas Transportation Ten Year Statement*, the National Grid; December 2005.

an estimated regulatory asset base of GBP 2.5 billion as of April 2005. From March 2007, price control formulas for gas and electricity transmission will be aligned.

For the low-pressure gas distribution lines, there are eight gas distribution networks that are owned by four gas distribution companies. Information on these networks is shown in Table 23.

There are currently nine major gas storage sites in Great Britain, including Rough, Hornsea and the five LNG facilities that were originally owned and operated by British Gas, plc. In addition, there are multiple diurnal storage tanks which are used to balance shifts in demand within a single 24-hour period. The diurnal facilities offer relatively modest storage volumes (1.5% of the national total) but can withdraw quickly and thus represent a large share of the combined withdrawal rate for the country (28.5%) Information on all storage facilities is listed in Table 24.

Table

UK Gas Distribution Networks

Project	Owner	Length of pipeline (km)	# of customers ('000)
East of England	National Grid Gas	46 700	3 875
London	National Grid Gas	22 600	2 254
North West	National Grid Gas	33 600	2 656
West Midlands	National Grid Gas	23 200	1 919
North England	Northern Gas Networks	34 700	2 466
Scotland	Scotia Gas Networks	22 600	1 701
South England	Scotia Gas Networks	47 300	3 942
Wales & West	Wales & West Utilities	31 800	2 366
Total		262 500	21 179

Source: Gas distribution price control review, Initial consultation Ofgem (December 2005).

Table

Gas Storage Facilities in the UK

Facility	Owner	Size		Withdrawal rate	
		GWh	%	GWh/d	%
Rough	Centrica	30 344	76.2	455	21.6
Hatfield Moor	Scottish Power	1 260	3.2	55	2.6
Hornsea	SSE	3 495	8.8	195	9.3
Hole House	EDF	300	0.8	30	1.4
Five LNG terminals	National Grid	3 846	9.7	769	36.5
Diurnal storage	National Grid	600	1.5	600	28.5
Total		39 845		2 104	

Source: Centrica plc and Dynegy Storage Ltd and Dynegy Onshore Processing UK Ltd: A report on the merger situation; UK Competition Commission, August 2003.

MARKET REFORM AND COMPETITION

The UK has a highly competitive downstream gas market. All consumers, regardless of size, are allowed to choose their supplier. The legal framework for gas and electricity supply is set by the Gas Act 1986 and the Electricity Act 1989, which have subsequently been amended, particularly by the Utilities Act 2000. In its 2005 *Annual Report on the Implementation of the Gas and*

Electricity Internal Market, the European Commission noted that the UK was one of only five EU countries that had no major issues or obstacles to competition in the their gas markets.

All suppliers and customers have a right to equal access for both the high-pressure distribution lines owned and operated by the National Grid and the low-pressure network owned and operated by the local distribution companies. A list of the major gas suppliers and their market shares over time is given in the table below.

—————————————————————————— Table **25**
Supply Companies and Market Shares

Supplier	Dec-02	Jun-03	Dec-03	Jun-04	Dec-04	Jun-05	Sep-05
BGT	63%	62%	61%	59%	57%	53%	53%
Powergen	12%	12%	12%	12%	13%	14%	14%
SSE	6%	6%	7%	8%	8%	9%	10%
npower	9%	9%	9%	9%	9%	9%	9%
Scottish Power	5%	5%	6%	7%	8%	9%	9%
EDF Energy	5%	5%	5%	5%	5%	5%	5%
Others	0%	0%	0%	0%	0%	0%	0%

Source: Domestic Retail Market Report – September 2005, Ofgem.

Since the introduction of consumer choice in the 1990s, nearly 50% of all retail customers have switched from the incumbent suppliers. From October 2003 through September 2005, approximately 300 000 gas customers switched supplier monthly. This is equivalent to between 15% and 20% of the customer base switching annually.

NATURAL GAS PRICES AND TAXATION

UK prices for gas have historically been lower than prices in other IEA countries. In 2004, retail ex tax gas prices for households were 14% below the IEA average. For prices with all taxes included, UK household prices were 25% below the IEA average.[28] In 2004, retail ex tax prices for industry were 25% below the IEA average[29] and 24% below the average when all taxes were taken into account.

---

28. Excludes countries for which this information was not available: Australia, Belgium, Germany, Italy, Norway and Sweden.
29. Excludes countries for which this information was not available: Australia, Belgium, Denmark, Germany, Italy, Luxembourg, the Netherlands, Norway and Sweden.

Figure 28

Gas Prices in the UK and in Other Selected IEA Countries, 1980 to 2005

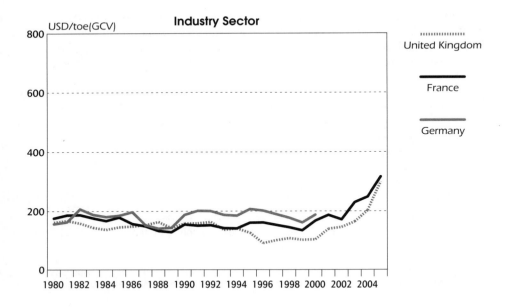

Industry Sector

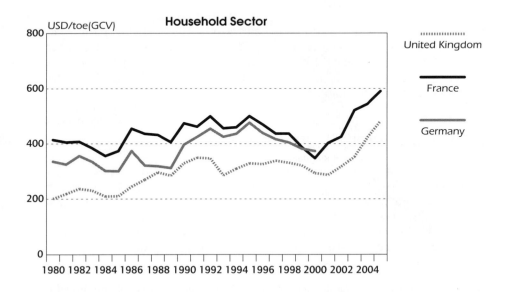

Household Sector

Source: *Energy Prices and Taxes*, IEA/OECD Paris, 2006.

Gas Prices in IEA Countries, 2005

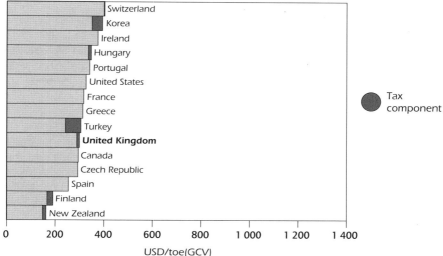

Industry Sector

Note: Tax information not available for the United States. Data not available for Australia, Austria, Belgium, Denmark, Germany, Italy, Japan, Luxembourg, the Netherlands, Norway and Sweden.

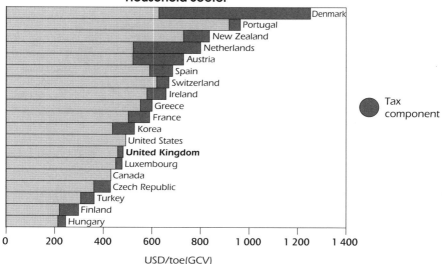

Household Sector

Note: Tax information not available for the United States. Data not available for Australia, Belgium, Germany, Italy, Japan, Norway and Sweden.

Source: *Energy Prices and Taxes*, IEA/OECD Paris, 2006.

Retail gas prices have risen substantially in recent years. Gas prices paid by average non-residential customers rose from 1.08 pence per kWh in the first quarter of 2004 to 1.97 pence per kWh in the fourth quarter of 2005, an increase of 83%.[30] Prices seen in the winter months of 2006 were lower than the fourth quarter of 2005. For residential customers, the retail price of gas rose by 33% from the first quarter of 2004 to the first quarter of 2006. Industrial customers tend to be more directly exposed to the wholesale market and thus will see the effects of changes in the wholesale gas price quicker than residential customers.

WINTER 2005/06

The UK gas market underwent a period of supply-demand tightness in the winter 2005/06. This caused high prices and a number of price spikes which sent the price of gas to record high levels. For much of the winter, UK wholesale gas prices were above 10 USD per MBtu and price spikes even reached 30 USD per MBtu in November 2005 and March 2006. In March 2006, National Grid issued an emergency warning on gas availability although at no point was gas supply to any customers involuntarily curtailed. The figure below shows maximum supply to the UK and projected demand under different weather scenarios.

Figure 30

Supply-Demand for Winter 2005/06

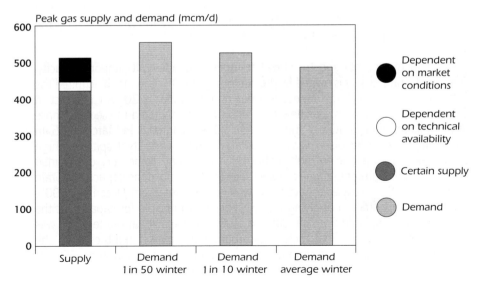

Source: *Natural Gas Market Review*, IEA/OECD Paris, 2006.

---

30. All prices in this chapter come from the March 2006 DTI *Quarterly Energy Prices* publication.

Weather during the winter of 2005/06 was mild-to-average and thus demand was actually lower than projected in Figure 30 for the "average winter" scenario. Also, consumption was affected by high market prices. Decrease in demand, primarily by the large users (*i.e.* factories and power plants), was observed.

Since demand was actually less than the average expected, the market tightness came almost entirely from a reduction in expected supply. A number of factors contributed to this reduction. One, domestic gas production declined more rapidly than envisioned by either the government or industry. Two, gas imports from the Continent via the Zeebrugge-Bacton interconnector were less than anticipated given the substantial price discrepancy between the two markets. Throughout the winter, UK prices were substantially above the apparent continental prices, but the interconnector was only operated at full load on two days. From 8 November 2005 through 31 March 2006, the interconnector was used at only 52% of maximum capacity. Why this arbitrage opportunity was not fully exploited by the continental gas players remains a matter of debate. Some observers have suggested that the continental onshore pipeline network was insufficient to get gas to Zeebrugge. Others have suggested that continental players were worried about their own customers' security of supply and, therefore, kept their own storage full rather than benefit from profitable sales into the UK. Others feel the general disparity between the UK's competitive gas market and the Continent's more centralised gas sector impedes any substantial arbitrage trading of the sort expected. The apparent failure of the continental gas players to respond to market signals and arbitrage opportunities has caused the UK government to file a complaint with the European Commission on the functioning of markets on the Continent.

Another factor contributing to market tightness was idle LNG import capacity. The Isle of Grain facility is owned by the National Grid. BP/Sonatrach acquired the first phase of 3.3 million tonnes LNG per annum under a 20-year contract in October 2003; Sonatrach, Gaz de France and Centrica acquired the second phase of 6.5 million tonnes LNG per annum under 20-year contracts in March 2005. In early winter, the facility often was not used at maximum capacity despite very high UK prices. This was due to high global LNG prices and some very determined buyers in other countries as well as reluctance by BP to make the capacity of Grain available to other companies, even if it was not using it. From December 2005, Ofgem was very strict in applying the use-it-or-lose-it principle for capacity at the Grain LNG terminal and from mid-January 2006 the capacity at the terminal was almost fully utilised. A final factor exacerbating the market tightness was the explosion at the Rough gas storage facility – accounting for more than 75% of total UK storage – which took a valuable supply option off-line.

Figure 31 below shows actual gas imports to the UK from both the continental interconnector and the Grain LNG facility versus total possible imports. It also shows the UK gas price over the same period for the sake of comparison.

Figure **31**

Import Capacity Underutilised during UK Price Hikes

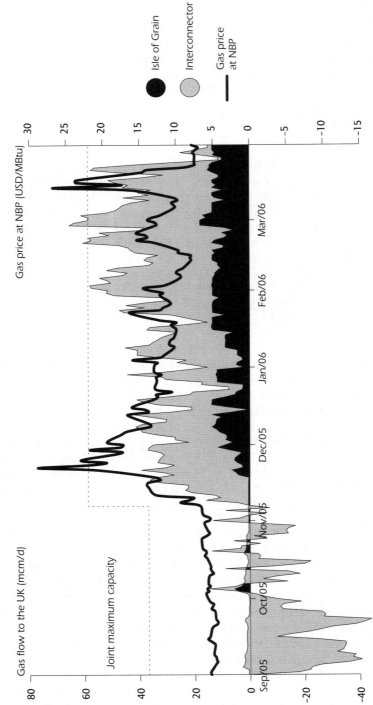

Source: *Natural Gas Market Review*, IEA/OECD Paris, 2006.

CRITIQUE

Fossil fuels dominate and will almost certainly continue to dominate the UK energy sector in the near and mid-term. In 2004, coal, gas and oil combined for 89.2% of TPES and this share is expected to grow to 90.4% of TPES by 2020. Fossil fuels accounted for 75.9% of all electricity generation in 2004 and are projected to account for 79.7% in 2020. Thus, even under the most aggressive renewables, energy efficiency and nuclear policies, fossil fuels will remain crucial to the UK's energy future.

The UK government is to be commended for its fossil fuel energy policy of the last decade. In the coal sector, completion of subsidy removal has brought market forces and market efficiency to the domestic mining sector without threats to security of energy supply. The government has managed gas and oil production in the North Sea without undue interference in private-sector activities. This production has provided a financial boon for the producers (UK and international), economic development for many regions bordering the North Sea, substantial taxes at national and local levels, and enhanced energy security. Furthermore, it now exports much of that technology and expertise worldwide. Finally, the UK has been a pioneer in the development of competitive downstream gas market and has reaped the benefits from this market reform for over ten years.

This decrease in production has had, and will continue to have, a significant impact on the UK energy sector. This is particularly true for gas which, unlike oil, has more of a regional than a global market. Increasing import reliance of gas raises energy security concerns as both the infrastructure and the "molecules" must be secured to supplant domestic production. Greater imports will also change the domestic pricing paradigm. UK gas prices will shift from being a mostly "UK price" driven by domestic supply and demand to being increasingly affected by external forces such as the global LNG market which is heavily influenced by the US gas market and continental gas pricing, which is heavily influenced by the world oil market.

However, this transition to greater import reliance need not cause substantial problems for the UK and in no ways calls for major shifts in policy. There are a number of steps the government can and should take to facilitate a smooth transition. The first concerns the provision of sound reliable data on the current and future North Sea production. The market tightness and resulting high prices and security of supply concerns during the winter of 2005/06 came in part from an unexpectedly fast decline in North Sea gas production. Largely on the basis of data collated and published by DTI and the National Grid, industry and policy makers alike were counting on more UK gas flowing into the domestic market than was actually the case. If industry had been able to accurately anticipate domestic production for this period, they likely would have begun infrastructure projects earlier to take advantage of the high prices.

On the demand side, gas users could have better prepared themselves for fuel switching. DTI maintains a database of information on producing fields, based on data provided by the operators. Projections of future production are inherently uncertain and operators may not necessarily be motivated to provide the most accurate forecast. However, with greater resources – and perhaps expanded legal rights to request data – DTI could more actively evaluate the numbers received from producers and then provide more reliable data on expected future production. This would allow industry and government to respond accordingly and thus help avoid the type of supply-demand tightness experienced in the winter 2005/06.

The North Sea crude oil and natural gas fields are mature and while there may be occasional upswings, production is clearly trending downward. The government should take all steps to provide the proper fiscal and regulatory environment to encourage continued domestic production. The new licences intended to motivate more exploration in promising frontier areas and by smaller producers are well conceived and will have some positive effect. The government should continue looking for ways to extend production, possibly in the area of enhanced oil recovery/CO_2 sequestration. Norway provides several good examples of policies to promote and extend oil and gas production. These include incentives for new producers to enter the market, partnerships with industry, marketing their fields to prospective investors and a programme to facilitate the transfer of declining fields and infrastructure from larger to smaller operators.

At the same time, there is only so much such policies can achieve. Production is a global business and producing companies will of course gravitate to the most promising fields with the best prospects at the lowest costs. Thus, in competing for the producers' interests, the UK must maximise its advantages, perhaps the greatest of which is its political and fiscal stability. The recently launched dialogue with industry to minimise surprises and ensure that any changes in the taxation or regulation can be anticipated well in advance is a positive development. On the other hand, the tax increase on producers that the government enacted in the past year could have a deleterious effect on future production. While this change in tax rates is understandable given the high prices and the government's commitment to a balance between oil consumers and producers. Stability and certainty in the fiscal regime is in the best interest of all parties and offers the most likely way to ensure continued production.

Greater imports will require greater import infrastructure in the form of pipelines and LNG terminals. During the winter 2005/06, the UK would have benefited from more import options. In that sense, the market failed to anticipate the supply-demand tightness and get the infrastructure built in time to take advantage of the high UK prices. However, the circumstances surrounding the winter 2005/06 were exceptional, a confluence of events that were difficult to predict. A tremendous amount of infrastructure will be brought on line in the coming years. Even if a portion of all the pipelines and LNG facilities planned and under construction is completed, there should be sufficient import capacity to handle the country's growing import reliance. Nevertheless, the government is still wise to follow the supply-demand balance and give warning if it looks like the market is getting too tight.

The one area where the infrastructure has not yet been sufficiently built is gas storage. Large storage facilities were not needed in the past because domestic producers could simply adjust flows from their fields to meet increased demand. Now that this flexibility is insufficient to meet peak winter demand, seasonal storage units will play a crucial role. Such facilities can store gas in the summer when demand is low and release in the winter while demand is high. The UK's one major gas storage facility, Rough, is not sufficient for the country's needs. In addition, the fire experienced at Rough in February 2006 demonstrated the imprudence of relying on a single major storage facility for the whole country. The current large discrepancy between winter and summer prices provide a strong market incentive for more storage plants to be built and a number of private companies have made plans to do so. However, these plans have been hampered to a great extent by local opposition and a general failure to gain planning consents. The government's May 2006 announcement that it would take measures to allow gas storage facilities to be constructed is a step in the right direction. Every effort should be made to ensure undue obstacles do not impede the construction of badly needed storage facilities.

During the Emergency Response Review of the UK in November 2003, the review team expressed its concern that UK oil companies would in future rely more on the reservation of oil stocks, using short-term contracts called "tickets" abroad under bilateral agreements to meet international stockholding obligations. As discussed within the context of the Standing Group on Emergency Questions (SEQ), there are concerns about availability in times of need when using short-term tickets held abroad.

The UK government has demonstrated its seriousness to meet its present and future international stockholding obligations as well as its continuing support for IEA emergency response policies and procedures. Nevertheless, the Emergency Response review team strongly recommended that the government also carry out a cost/benefits analysis of an agency-type of system which would guarantee credible, accountable and quickly accessible stocks in times of crisis and would assist industry in meeting the government's future international obligations as the UK becomes a net importer of oil and oil products.

The downstream distribution and retail sector for natural gas works well. There is a plurality of suppliers resulting in competition for large and small customers alike. There have been no accusations of market power abuse, or suggestions that suppliers have not been granted true equal access to pipelines. The UK is to be commended for its downstream gas market which can serve as a model for other countries.

RECOMMENDATIONS

The government of the United Kingdom should:

▶ *Increase resources to provide reports on the crude oil and natural gas sectors, particularly on the likely future production, to provide the best possible signal to investors in the gas supply infrastructure.*

▶ *Ensure an upstream fiscal regime that stresses predictability in order to meet the twin goals of promoting investment and achieving a balance between oil producers and the country's interest.*

▶ *Examine the conditions required to encourage more natural gas storage, removing obstacles as much as possible, given the growing import dependence and the expected increase in gas-fired electricity generation.*

NUCLEAR GENERATING FLEET

There are 23 nuclear units in operation in the United Kingdom on 9 sites (see Table 26). The nuclear power plants are operated by British Energy (BE), the largest electricity generator of the country, and BNFL, a state-owned company which is also engaged in nuclear fuel cycle service activities. British Energy operates 14 Advanced Gas Reactors (AGR) and one Pressurised Water Reactor (PWR), Sizewell B; it also operates a large coal-fired power plant. BNFL operates eight Gas Cooled Reactors (Magnox). Except Sizewell B, connected to the grid in 1995, the nuclear units in operation in the UK were commissioned between 1965 and 1988. The nuclear fleet is ageing and, owing to the uniqueness of the reactor types (with the exception of Sizewell B), there is limited international experience on plant life management.

———————————————— Table

Nuclear Power Plants in Operation, 2006

Name		Type	Net capacity, MWe	Grid connection	Published lifetime	Operator
Dungeness	A2	Magnox	2 x 225	1965	2006	BNFL
	B1/B2	AGR	2 x 555	1983/1985	2018	AGR
Hartlepool	A1/A2	AGR	2 x 605	1983/1984	2014	BE
Heysham	A1/B1	AGR	2 x 575	1983/1984	2014	BE
Heysham	A2/B2	AGR	2 x 625	1988	2023	BE
Hinkley Point	B1/B2	AGR	2 x 610	1976	2011	BE
Hunterston	B1/B2	AGR	2 x 595	1976/1977	2011	BE
Oldbury	A1/A2	Magnox	2 x 217	1967/1968	2008	BNFL
Sizewell	A1/A2	Magnox	2 x210	1966/1968	2006	BNFL
	B	PWR	1188	1995	2035	BE
Torness	1/2	AGR	2 x 625	1988/1989	2023	BE
Wylfa	1/2	Magnox	2 x 490	1971	2010	BNFL

Sources: IAEA and Energy Policy Review Consultation.

Figure

Capacity of Nuclear Fleet Based on Published Lifetimes

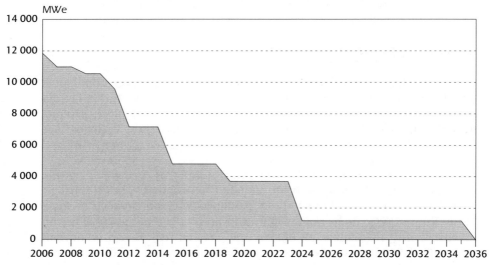

Sources: International Atomic Energy Agency and Energy Policy Review Consultation.

The average availability factors of the UK nuclear power plants remain rather low as compared to those currently reached in other OECD countries and worldwide.[31] However, fleet availability has been improving and, as a result, nuclear electricity generation has increased in the last ten years while its share of total generation has remained stable. Today, nuclear energy supplies some 20% of the UK electricity consumption (20.6% in 2005).

NUCLEAR INDUSTRY STRUCTURE

Prior to 1996, all UK nuclear plants were owned by the State. In 1996, British Energy – with ownership of eight power stations – was privatised, raising GBP 1.2 billion for the government. A group of older plants which did not draw sufficient investor interest – the Magnox plants – were put into a company called Magnox Electric. Those Magnox plants remain state-owned through British Nuclear Fuels (BNFL).

In 2002, shares of British Energy (BE) tumbled by 90% as a result of cost overruns, sharp decreases in UK wholesale power prices and the Climate Change Levy introduced in April 2000 which cost British Energy

---

31. According to the IAEA statistics, the average energy availability factor of UK reactors during the period 2002-2004 is 75.2%, compared with 82.6% worldwide.

GBP 80 million to GBP 100 million per year. In the autumn of 2002, the government stepped in and provided a loan to the company to keep it solvent. The move was criticised and there was talk of BE moving into administration (*i.e.* declaring bankruptcy). Nevertheless, the government proceeded with a loan of GBP 655 million to "provide working capital for the business and collateral". Since that time, however, the company's fortunes have improved substantially. UK wholesale power prices have risen and the company struck a deal with creditors. In addition, the government agreed to shift some decommissioning costs away from BE and take responsibility for certain liabilities associated with the plants. All this puts BE on a much stronger footing. Since relisting on the stock exchange in January 2005, BE shares have risen by more than 250%.

The UK has a well-established nuclear industry, covering all the steps of the fuel cycle with the exception of uranium production. The URENCO[32] enrichment plant, using the centrifuge technology, has a capacity of some 3 400 tSWU[33] per year. BNFL operates a conversion plant at Springfields with a capacity of 6 000 tonnes of uranium per year as well as fuel fabrication plants for various reactor designs with a total capacity of 1 500 tonnes of heavy metal per year. It also operates reprocessing facilities for spent fuels from UK reactors (Magnox and AGR) and from foreign light water reactors. There is no domestic industrial capability for the design and construction of nuclear power plants.

REGULATORY FRAMEWORK AND RELATIONSHIP OF THE REGULATOR

The Secretary of State for Trade and Industry is accountable to Parliament for safety at nuclear power stations and other licensed civil nuclear sites in the UK. He is advised on nuclear safety issues by the independent Health and Safety Commission (HSC) which has statutory responsibility for ensuring that there is an adequate framework for regulation of safety at nuclear sites in the UK. The licensing and day-to-day inspection is carried out by the Health and Safety Executive's Nuclear Installations Inspectorate (HSE) which regulates nuclear safety under licences with conditions covering the design, construction, operation, maintenance and decommissioning of nuclear installations. The HSC and the HSE are accountable to the Secretary of State for Trade and Industry for their nuclear safety work.

---

32. Urenco is a joint Anglo-Dutch-German company owning and operating three enrichment plants, one in each country, all using the centrifuge technology.
33. Separative work unit, the measure of capacity for enrichment plants.

WASTE MANAGEMENT AND DISPOSAL

Regarding radioactive waste management and disposal, most low-level waste (LLW) is currently disposed of at the state-owned LLW repository near Drigg in Cumbria, which was licensed to BNFL and has been in operation since 1959. Intermediate-level waste is stored, mostly at the sites of nuclear facilities in operation, and eventually will be disposed of in a dedicated repository. The Committee on Radioactive Waste Management (CoRWM), created in 2003, is appointed by the government to review the options for managing radioactive wastes. They are to recommend the option, or combination of options, that provides a long-term solution which protects people and the environment. After a period of consultations with experts and stakeholders, CoRWM released its recommendations to the government in July 2006. These are discussed below in the section on Future Nuclear Plants.

PLANT DECOMMISSIONING

The Nuclear Decommissioning Authority (NDA), set up in April 2005 under the Energy Act 2004, is responsible for the decommissioning and clean-up of state-owned civil nuclear sites in the UK, in safe, secure and cost-effective ways that protect the environment and future generations. The NDA owns the plant and facilities of BNFL (owner of the Magnox stations) at Sellafield, THORP/Sellafield mixed-oxide fuel plant and Springfields, and took responsibility for managing the clean-up of the United Kingdom Atomic Energy Authority (UKAEA) sites. This all flowed from transfer schemes under the Energy Act 2004. BNFL and UKAEA were restructured so that they now operate these facilities, both for clean-up and continuing commercial operations, under contract to the NDA rather than as principals. In due course, the intention is that clean-up of sites will be subject to competition.

The liabilities passed on to NDA are public-sector legacy because the facilities were state-owned and the liability funds accumulated during their operation were managed at the state level. At the end of 2005, total liabilities were expected to be GBP 56 billion. However, the NDA released a report on 30 March 2006 with new figures for nuclear clean-up costs. It is estimated that it will cost GBP 62.7 billion with GBP 7.5 billion in potential extra costs to clean contaminated land. The NDA noted that these estimates included a "range of factors... which will require further assessment". The plan is to establish the full costs for clean-up by 2008.

The NDA has a budget of GBP 2.2 billion; half funded by grant-in-aid, the other half from commercial income from its productive sites. Over time the contribution from income will fall off as productive units are progressively taken out of service. The UK government has accepted public responsibility for funding the clean-up and decommissioning of this nuclear legacy.

Since its restructuring, BE no longer bears the full financial risk of its liabilities. The government has agreed to meet the costs associated with discharging its historic spent AGR fuel (pre-14 January 2005) and to underwrite BE's segregated decommissioning fund (which will fund BE's decommissioning costs and certain uncontracted liabilities). BE will remain responsible for managing its decommissioning but the NDA will review and approve its decommissioning plans and also approve payments out of the segregated fund to BE.

FUTURE NUCLEAR PLANTS

The 2003 Energy White Paper states that nuclear power's "current economics make it an unattractive option for new, carbon-free generating capacity and there are also important issues of nuclear waste to be resolved". However, the Paper also states that the government does "not rule out the possibility that at some point in the future new nuclear build might be necessary" but that a thorough public consultation would be needed before pursuing any new nuclear generation. In its second annual report on the implementation of the 2003 White Paper (July 2005), the government restates its position that nuclear may be necessary at some point in the future but that "the fullest public consultation" would be needed before any new nuclear plants are built.

In March 2006, the Sustainable Development Commission (SDC)[34] released a report on the desirability of continued UK nuclear generation.[35] In the report, it concludes that "there is no justification for bringing forward plans for a new nuclear power programme at this time." At the same time, the report does not advocate prohibiting private actors from building new nuclear plants although it doubts this will happen without government support. The SDC cites five disadvantages for nuclear: i) lack of available solution for long-term waste; ii) high cost and cost uncertainty; iii) inflexibility; iv) undermining of energy efficiency; and v) international security risks.

The Energy Review in its July 2006 report, *The Energy Challenge*, also addresses nuclear power. The report states that nuclear power "is an important source of low carbon electricity in the UK" and that "new nuclear power stations would make a significant contribution to meeting [the country's] energy policy goals". This more positive assessment of nuclear *vis-à-vis* the 2003 White Paper is prompted by higher projected fossil fuel prices and the introduction of a carbon price.

---

34. The Sustainable Development Commission is the government's independent watchdog on sustainable development, reporting to the Prime Minister and the First Ministers of Scotland and Wales.
35. "The role of nuclear power in a low-carbon economy", March 2006.

The Energy Review report announces a number of steps the government intends to take that would remove barriers to the development of new nuclear capacity. These include: setting out a proposed framework for the consideration of issues relevant to planning and new nuclear build; providing the basis for long-term waste management; and developing guidance for potential promoters of new nuclear stations. The treatment of long-term waste management was more directly addressed in a report by the Committee on Radioactive Waste Management (CoRWM), an independent group appointed in 2003 by the government. The report, *Managing our Radioactive Waste Safely*, published on 31 July 2006, includes a set of recommendations which CoRWM regards as an interdependent package. The recommendations are:

- In the long term, disposal of radioactive waste deep underground, an option known as geological disposal.

- Robust interim storage, in recognition of the fact that the process leading to the creation of suitable facilities for disposal may take several decades.

- An equal partnership between government and potential host communities based on a willingness to participate.

- The immediate creation of an independent oversight body to oversee the process of implementation.

While the government will be responsible for managing existing waste, the Energy Review report makes clear that the initiative, development and financing of any new nuclear plants would not be the job of the State. The report says that "any new nuclear plants would be proposed, developed, constructed and operated by the private sector, who would also meet full decommissioning costs and their full share of long-term waste management costs".

CRITIQUE

While the nuclear units in operation have demonstrated increasingly good technical and economic performance in the context of the liberalised UK electricity market, no new unit has been ordered since the late 1980s and Sizewell B, the last unit to be built, was connected to the grid in 1995. The nuclear industry remains active in several domains of the fuel cycle but there is no domestic capability for reactor design and construction. In spite of the decision of the UK government to join Generation IV International Forum (GIF), the public nuclear R&D effort is extremely low, in line with the national policy to rely on the industry for RD&D.

The nuclear power plants are ageing and a number of units will be retired in the near future. In 2006, two Magnox stations, Dungeness A and Sizewell A, are to be closed. Although several AGRs will likely be operated beyond their expected lifetime (closure by 2020-2025), only Sizewell B (1.2 GWe) will remain on line after 2030. In light of the role nuclear plays in reducing UK carbon emissions, it would be advisable for the government to develop a strategy for substituting retired nuclear power plants by carbon-free options (*e.g.* energy efficiency, non-intermittent renewable sources or coal-fired plants with carbon capture and sequestration) or new nuclear units.

Nuclear, like all generating choices, has its advantages and disadvantages. Consistent with the UK's market-oriented philosophy, the choice on how much, if any, nuclear capacity is to be built should be left to market players. Government's primary role is to ensure that all costs of nuclear operation are seen clearly by these market players when they make their decisions, and to inform the public about the alternatives, which in this case would most likely be increased reliance on gas imports for power generation. This would include the benefits of nuclear coming from reduced GHG emissions and liabilities related to decommissioning and long-term waste storage. The government adopted this approach in its treatment of nuclear by the Energy Review.

Additional necessary government roles for nuclear power include:

- Establishing the framework for the treatment of interim and long-term waste disposal from new and existing plants.

- Establishing the framework for decommissioning new and existing plants.

- Helping to select a site for a long-term waste storage facility.

- Establishing a licensing process for new nuclear power plants in line with current international best practices.

- Continual monitoring of safe operations at all nuclear plants.

The Energy Review's July 2006 report and the work of the CoRWM begin to clarify how the government will play these roles. However, the work done and the proposals made thus far do not yet include sufficient information on the exact steps the government would take. While defining the general structure of the government's role is essential, further work needs to be done to fill in the details. Without such additional work, potential investment in new nuclear generating stations still face substantial uncertainty which will act as a barrier to new plant.

Any possible new nuclear plants must be preceded by a clear plan for "legacy issues", namely decommissioning and waste treatment for existing plants. International experience shows that a robust national policy for the disposal of all types of radioactive waste is essential to ensure public confidence in nuclear energy and to allow operators of nuclear facilities to internalise fully the costs associated with back-end activities. The number of nuclear facilities in operation, or already shut down, in the country calls for a rapid move towards the selection and implementation of a comprehensive national policy for radioactive waste disposal. Given that the amounts needed for decommissioning and waste storage are uncertain (see the UK's recent increase in clean-up estimates), it is best to err on the side of caution. Furthermore, it is essential that the government put in place schemes to ensure that adequate funds will be available to cover expenses associated with the decommissioning of all nuclear facilities and the disposal of all types of waste. Industry should accumulate the funds according to the polluter pays principle. Funds should be accumulated by the polluter/user of electricity, and the government should monitor the accuracy of estimated costs and the adequacy and management of the funds. The July 2006 CoRWM report is a step in the right direction but must now be supplemented with more concrete work, in particular selection of a site for nuclear waste disposal.

The government recently created the Nuclear Decommissioning Authority (NDA), in charge of designing and implementing a strategy for the decommissioning of state-owned nuclear facilities (power plants and fuel cycle facilities). This decision is commendable, although it probably should have been taken much earlier. It is important that NDA demonstrates its capability to address issues raised by historic liabilities in a safe and cost-effective manner and to create a reliable framework allowing the operators of nuclear facilities in service to plan and finance their eventual decommissioning.

As in many other OECD countries, the United Kingdom is experiencing rapid ageing of manpower in the field of nuclear energy. The operation and maintenance of existing nuclear facilities and the control of their safety require highly-qualified manpower. Even if no new nuclear power plants are built in the country, industrial activities will continue for several decades taking into account the remaining lifetime of the plants in operation and the lead times for decommissioning and waste management prior to their final disposal.

The nuclear education and R&D policy of the government would benefit from enhanced coherence and consistency with the requirements of the existing nuclear installations. It is important to ensure adequate education and training opportunities for replacing the ageing workforce in the nuclear energy sector. In the light of the number and variety of nuclear facilities in operation in the country, it might be desirable also to design and implement fundamental R&D programmes. Such programmes are relevant to support innovation that might be developed further by the industry and to attract young talented researchers who will replace the ageing workforce.

RECOMMENDATIONS

The government of the United Kingdom should:

▶ *Clarify the UK position regarding nuclear energy and, if applicable, establish a legal and regulatory framework for potential investors to assess with a reasonable degree of confidence the short- and long-term risks and benefits of building a new nuclear unit.*

▶ *Define a national policy covering the disposal of all types of radioactive waste and take steps towards its implementation to allow the industry to assess and fully internalise corresponding costs for existing and, if applicable, future nuclear power plants and fuel cycle facilities.*

▶ *Provide a robust and stable scheme for the accumulation, management and control of a fund for covering future financial liabilities (decommissioning and waste disposal) for existing and, if applicable, future nuclear power plants and fuel cycle facilities.*

▶ *Assess the adequacy of education and training for developing the human resources/qualified manpower needed to ensure the safe operation and decommissioning of existing nuclear units and, if applicable, the licensing and operation of new units.*

ENERGY RESEARCH AND DEVELOPMENT (R&D)

ENERGY R&D POLICY OBJECTIVES

UK public sector investments in energy research are linked to the four key policy goals set out in the 2003 Energy White Paper:

- To put the country on a path to cut the UK's CO_2 emissions by some 60% by about 2050, with real progress by 2020.
- To maintain the reliability of energy supplies.
- To promote competitive markets in the UK and beyond, helping to raise the rate of sustainable economic growth and to improve UK productivity.
- To ensure that every home is adequately and affordably heated.

Besides these key policy goals, some of the main drivers for change in the UK energy sector, including priority setting for research and development are:

- UK becomes a net gas and oil importer.
- Concerns over security of supply and climate change.
- Gas and nuclear generating capacity needs replacement.

A key challenge defined by the UK government during the review process is how to maintain and encourage innovation while maintaining UK principles of non-intervention.

STAKEHOLDERS

The main stakeholders in UK energy research and development are (but not exclusively):

- Government departments:
  - Department of Trade and Industry (DTI) – leads on energy supply.
  - Department of Transport (DfT) – leads on transport.
  - Defra – leads on climate change and energy efficiency.
  - Office of Deputy Prime Minister (ODPM) – leads on the built environment.
- Research Councils – leads on basic research.
- UK Energy Research Centre (UKERC).
- Carbon Trust, Energy Savings Trust.
- Regional Development Agencies.
- Devolved administrations.

- Universities.
- Industry – companies and representative organisations.
- Consumers and consumer groups.

Below is an overview of the UK energy research landscape showing research entities and programmes involved in basic research, applied research, demonstration and deployment, and international collaboration for various technology groupings.

———————————————— Figure **33**

Overview of UK Energy Research Landscape

	Basic/applied strategic	Applied	D&D	International
Demand	Carbon Vision, UKERC	Defra, DfT ODPM, CT	Carbon Trust	REEEP
Conventional energy	EPSRC responsive, TSEC	HSE, Defra	ITI-Energy, NaREC	CSLF, GEN IV, M2M
Future sources	SUPERGEN, Fusion, TSEC, UKERC	Technology Programme, Carbon Trust	ITI, RDAs, CT, DTI Capital Grants	REEEP
Infrastructure	TSEC, SUPERGEN, DG Centre, UKERC	Technical architecture	ITI-Energy	IPHE
Socio-economic	TSEC, UKERC	Defra, DfT		

Source: UK Energy Research Centre, 2006.

STAKEHOLDERS IN PRIORITY SETTING AND PROGRAMME MANAGEMENT

No single organisation has overall responsibility for energy research. Priorities are set by individual organisations within the context of their activities and needs. Main stakeholders in energy R&D policy formulation, priority setting and programme management are DTI, Defra, Research Councils (especially the Engineering and Physical Sciences Research Council), the Energy Research Partnership, the UK Energy Research Centre and the Carbon Trust.

DTI

Government policy on research is co-ordinated by the Office of Science and Technology (OST) which is embedded in the Department of Trade and Industry (DTI); the Secretary of State for Trade and Industry is the Cabinet Minister with overall responsibility for the government's science policy. The OST is headed by the government's Chief Scientific Advisor (CSA) who provides advice to the government on Science Engineering and Technology (SET). In addition to its cross-departmental role in advising government, the OST has a major function in administering funds to the Research Councils.

Energy Research Partnership

The Energy Research Partnership was established in 2005 to give strategic direction to UK energy RD&D, in the context of the government's Energy White Paper and its overall aim to increase national research and development expenditure. It is chaired by Sir David King and Paul Golby (E.ON) and brings together key funders of energy research and innovation from government, industry and academia. The objective is to promote a coherent approach and to enhance prospects for attracting increasing energy-related investments and activity.

The Engineering and Physical Sciences Research Council (EPSRC)

The Research Councils are the main public investors in basic research in the UK with interests ranging from biomedicine and particle physics to the environment, engineering and economic research.

EPSRC is a non-departmental governmental public body, funded by the government through the Department of Trade and Industry's Office of Science and Technology. It is one of eight Research Councils funded by the government and works collectively with those councils on issues of common concern via Research Councils UK. Research Council funding is largely allocated in grants to universities (which are public institutions) and to Research Council Institutes, where most public-sector research is carried out. The universities come under the Department for Education and Skills (DfES) which is responsible for providing the basic infrastructure for carrying out the research; this bimodal scheme is referred to as the dual support system. The Research Councils also provide large facilities for research by university scientists, and subscriptions to international research organisations.

UK Energy Research Centre (UKERC)

The UK Energy Research Centre (UKERC) was established in 2004 following a recommendation from the 2002 Review of Energy initiated by Sir David King, the UK government's Chief Scientific Advisor. The UK Energy Research Centre's mission is to be the UK's pre-eminent centre of research and source of authoritative information and leadership on sustainable energy systems. The role of the UKERC includes conducting research *and* co-ordinating a National Energy Research Network. UKERC is funded by three Research Councils: the Engineering and Physical Sciences Research Council (EPSRC), the

Natural Environment Research Council (NERC) and the Economic and Social Research Council (ESRC).

UKERC is a distributed centre operated by a consortium of eight universities and research institutions organised around demand reduction (Oxford); future sources of energy (Edinburgh); infrastructure and supply (Manchester); systems and modelling (PSI); environmental sustainability (CEH, Lancaster); and materials (Imperial College).

This centre was announced by the Chancellor in the 2006 Budget and is intended to be fully operational from early 2008. The government has committed GBP 500 million to the Energy Technology Institute (ETI) over 10 years and is looking for the same commitment from the private sector. If this is achieved, ETI will be a 50/50 public/private sector organisation delivering R&D to accelerate the development of low-carbon energy technologies (non-nuclear) that can be deployed commercially. It represents a significant increase in funding and strategic direction.

In addition to this framework, there is a range of advisory bodies and other non-government institutions. At the centre of government, the Cabinet Office reports to the Prime Minister, receiving advice from the Council for Science and Technology (a group of eminent individuals from government, industry and academia), as well as that from the Chief Scientific Adviser.

Defra and Carbon Trust

The Carbon Trust, an independent company established and funded by Defra, has significant programmes to promote low-carbon technology development at all stages of the innovation spectrum, from early stage research through to promoting deployment.

ENERGY R&D PRIORITIES

RD&D POLICY REVIEW

The last formal, overarching identification of priorities for energy research was the study of the Chief Scientific Adviser's Energy Research Review Group (ERRG) in 2001/02. The ERRG considered whether the overall level of expenditure on research, development and demonstration (RD&D) was sufficient, whether it was being targeted on the right areas and who should in future maintain an overview of expenditure.

The ERRG agreed that increased RD&D effort was crucial to identifying new energy options which would deliver a secure and sustainable supply of energy with substantially lower carbon emissions. The group recommended that energy research and its proper co-ordination should be key priorities for government, and that UK's spending on RD&D should be raised to bring it more in line with that of its nearest EU competitors. Consideration should be given to setting up a dedicated national energy research centre and a suitable body should be entrusted with the mission of collecting and co-ordinating information on energy RD&D. The following key RD&D priority areas were identified to ensure a sustainable energy supply with lower carbon emissions:

- Further strategic investigation into non-technical policy drivers, with particular attention to understanding the market context into which new technology is deployed.
- Sufficient focus on basic research activities.
- More cross-boundary research.
- Six key technology areas of scientific research:
  - CO_2 sequestration.
  - Energy efficiency.
  - Hydrogen production and storage.
  - Nuclear power (nuclear waste).
  - Solar photovoltaic.
  - Wave and tidal power.

The findings of the ERRG were endorsed in the 2003 Energy White Paper.

The government's current Energy Review planned to reconsider issues surrounding energy research and innovation strategy. However, the Review's initial report (published in July 2006) did not go into any details about research and development. The Review only listed some of the areas where the UK hopes to harness the potential of technology, namely:

- Improving the efficiency of the electricity system.
- Low-carbon transport systems.
- Nuclear fusion only.

The Energy Review also presented some background thinking about the National Institute of Energy Technologies. The Institute was announced by the Chancellor in the 2006 Budget.

GOVERNMENT SUPPORT FOR R&D

The UK government has developed a Technology Strategy, with a medium- to long-term perspective, which will provide a framework for setting policy priorities and improving the effectiveness of business support. The 2005 annual report of the Technology Strategy Board identified Emerging Energy Technologies as one of seven[36] key technology areas which underpin the UK economy.

The Technology Programme managed by the Department of Trade and Industry is funding at least GBP 20 million per annum to RD&D on Emerging Energy Technologies.

---

36. The seven areas were: Advanced Materials; Bioscience and Healthcare; Design Engineering and Advanced Manufacturing; Electronics and Photonics; Emerging Energy Technologies; Information and Communications Technology (ICT), Sustainable Production and Consumption.

Figure 34

Examples of Government Support to Low-carbon Energy Technologies at Each Stage of their Development

R&D
Basic research

– Research councils
programmes
(*e.g.* Supergen)

Development
Applied research

– **Technology Programme**

– OGD programmes

– Carbon Trust R&D Programme

– International R&D (IEA, EU)
Framework Programme, etc.

Demonstration
Early deployment of
emerging technologies

– Offshore wind capital
grants scheme

– Marine Renewables Fund

– Bioenergy capital
grants scheme

– Low Carbon Buildings
Programme

– Hydrogen and Carbon
Abatement Technology
Demonstration Fund

Pre-commercial
Moving towards
large-scale production

– Renewables Obligation

– Non Fossil Fuel Obligation

– Exemption from the Climate
Change Levy

The Technology Programme R&D is also critical to support (not directly funded) demonstration activity

The government also supports low-carbon technologies through non-financial support:
  – Reform of planning regulations for renewables (PPS 22)
  – Committee on Radioactive Waste Management
  – Leading international effort to establish regulations for CCS

Source: DTI, Energy Industries and Technologies Unit.

BREAKDOWN OF RESEARCH COUNCIL ENERGY INVESTMENTS BY TECHNOLOGY

Support for energy research and skills through the Research Councils – essentially at the "basic research" end of the spectrum – is expected to rise from GBP 40 m to over GBP 70 m per annum by 2007-08. Details of past investments by the Research Councils are given in the table below. The table shows that increased research priority has been given to the key technology areas identified by the Energy Research Review Group (CO_2 sequestration, energy efficiency, hydrogen production and storage, nuclear power, solar PV, and wave and tidal power). Furthermore Biomass, Networks and Conventional have received increased R&D funding from government.

—————————————————— Table **27**

Spending by Research Councils on Energy Technologies

	1997-8	1998-9	1999-00	2000-01	2001-2	2002-3	2003-4	2004-5
Biofuel	0	0	0	22	52	144	135	92
Biomass	447	871	736	601	701	783	1 043	1 186
CHP	4	36	63	77	267	357	226	71
CO_2 sequestration	0	0	0	23	42	78	30	42
Fuel cells	888	1 012	703	899	1 145	1 468	1 193	918
Hydrogen & other vectors	30	136	59	83	319	517	1 494	1 495
Solar	1 440	1 286	1 076	1 134	1 130	1 157	1 453	1 753
Photovoltaic	2 255	3 002	2 760	2 992	3 536	2 770	2 381	2 762
Wave & tidal	0	157	175	301	606	617	830	1 050
Wind	200	226	178	261	330	490	482	256
Waste	66	10	40	40	96	125	169	154
Geothermal	0	0	0	40	65	64	73	79
Storage	326	650	670	838	889	810	730	500
Networks	1 348	1 168	1 081	919	1 115	1 388	1 805	2 463
Other	0	49	49	128	28	28	28	28
Total renewable	**7 003**	**8 602**	**7 590**	**8 356**	**10 319**	**10 795**	**12 072**	**12 850**
Conventional	331	103	108	549	1 120	1 349	1 253	1 628
Fission power	42	81	62	128	325	307	212	125
Energy efficiency & low-carbon innovation	1 732	1 855	1 694	1 400	1 671	1 980	1 212	2 914
Other & general	0	13	303	670	602	665	762	1 944
Fusion ‡	16 600	12 600	14 300	17 000	14 400	14 600	15 630	19 530
Total	**25 708**	**23 254**	**24 056**	**28 104**	**28 438**	**29 697**	**31 141**	**38 992**

Source: Country submission.

DEPARTMENTAL SPENDING AND CARBON TRUST

Government departments fund energy R&D to varying degrees, with DTI the biggest funder. This includes significant capital grants for deployment of offshore wind (the current programme amounts to GBP 117 million), and demonstration funding for carbon abatement technologies (GBP 35 million), biomass (GBP 66 m) and marine technologies (GBP 50 m). Other departments tend to pursue research focusing more on their policy interests and involving smaller sums. The table below draws together information on the key government and Carbon Trust programmes covering low-carbon technologies:

Table 28

Government and Carbon Trust Programmes for Low-carbon Technologies

Programme	Technologies	Period	UK funding
DTI Technology Programme	Various	SR04 +	SR04 commitment to fund *at least* GBP 20 m p.a. to emerging energy technologies
Bioenergy Capital Grants	Bioenergy	Since 2002	GBP 66 m (joint with Big Lottery Fund)
Carbon Abatement Technologies (CAT) Strategy	Carbon capture and storage Clean coal technologies	2005-2015	GBP 20 m from 2005/06 to 2007/08 GBP 25 m capital grant 2006/07 to 2009/10 for demonstration project
Clear Skies Capital Grants Scheme	Renewables	2003-06	GBP 12.5 million
Energy Efficiency Technology Fund (Carbon Trust)	Various	2006/07 – 2007/08	GBP 20 million
Generation IV Research	Next generation of advanced nuclear reactors		GBP 4.3 m 2005/06 GBP 5 m 2006/07 GBP 5 m 2007/08
Hydrogen and Fuel Cells Technology	Hydrogen	2005/06 to 2008/09	GBP 15 m over the period forms part of a GBP 40 m package including carbon abatement technologies (see above)
Major PV Demonstration Programme	Photovoltaic	2002-06	GBP 31 m
Wave and Tidal Stream Energy Demonstration Programme	Wave and tidal stream	2006 onwards	GBP 42 m allocated to date from GBP 50 m budget
Offshore Wind Capital Grants	Round 1 offshore wind	Since 2002	GBP 117 m
Carbon Trust	Generating technologies and energy efficiency	Approx GBP 70 m funding p.a. from Defra	

Source: Country submission.

The government published its 10-Year Science and Innovation Investment Framework in July 2004. This presents the government's commitment to science and research over the next decade, with the long-term objective of increasing the overall levels of investment in research and development to 2.5% of GDP by 2014. In 2002 UK spending on R&D as a percentage of GDP was 1.86 (public spending 0.62 and private spending 1.24).

TRENDS IN UK GOVERNMENT SUPPORT FOR RD&D

UK RD&D budgets have declined dramatically since the 1980s. The decline reflects that, before the era of privatisation, the nationalised energy industries in the UK provided an important source of research effort. As a result of privatisation, this activity was transferred to the private sector. Whether it still continues, and the contribution it makes to UK's energy effort, is difficult to measure.

The UK government energy R&D budget per GDP is low compared to other important IEA countries, as seen from Figure 36.

NEW PROGRAMMES AND INITIATIVES

Towards a Sustainable Energy Economy (TSEC) is a "whole-systems" energy research programme which supports the UK Energy Research Centre (UKERC) with funds of GBP 13 m over five years. The UKERC, as well as undertaking its own programme of energy research, is drawing together a National Energy Research Network of UK expertise/researchers in energy research, thus providing a focal point for the UK energy research community. In addition, TSEC supports six research consortia covering Bioenergy; Carbon Management (to assess options for decoupling fossil fuel use from carbon emissions through carbon sequestration and storage); Keeping the Nuclear Option Open (with GBP 6 m over 4 years) and three addressing "Managing Uncertainties" and understanding energy demand, including understanding regulatory and market effects, public attitudes and energy emissions trading; research into Lifestyle, Values and Energy Consumption; and analysis and evaluation of policies to manage a transition to a sustainable energy economy.

Sustainable Power Generation and Supply (SuperGen) provides large-scale, consortium funding for the development of new and emerging energy technologies. Currently supporting 13 consortia (funded at GBP 2-4 m each over four years) on hydrogen, biomass and bioenergy, marine energy, future network technologies, photovoltaic materials, conventional power plant lifetime extension, fuel cells, highly distributed power systems, excitonic solar cells, energy storage, biological fuel cells, wind energy, and energy infrastructure. Possible ideas for further consortia include hydrogen production and microgeneration.

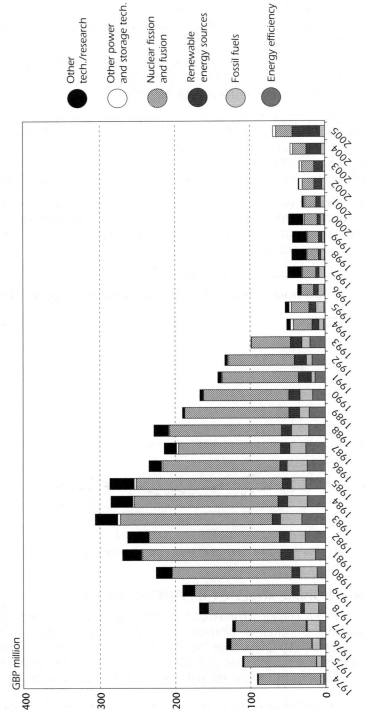

Figure 35

Government Energy RD&D Budgets, 1974 to 2005

GBP million

Other tech./research

Other power and storage tech.

Nuclear fission and fusion

Renewable energy sources

Fossil fuels

Energy efficiency

Source: Country submission.

EPSRC Science and Innovation award to University of Strathclyde for research into "Innovative Power Networks, Demand/Supply-side Integration and Nuclear Engineering".

"Nuclear Technology Education Consortium" (NTEC) with funding of around GBP 1 million from EPSRC to provide masters-level and continuing professional training for the nuclear industries.

An Engineering Doctorate Centre in Nuclear Engineering with funding of up to GBP 5 million from EPSRC, in collaboration with MoD, BE, BNFL, Nexia and AWE, to enhance the expertise base to address nuclear research issues (including materials development for high radiation flux situations, high-level waste control and management, and decommissioning nuclear facilities).

Carbon Vision (with a low carbon/energy efficiency focus) funded by EPSRC in association with the Carbon Trust, NERC & ESRC – including projects on low carbon buildings; life cycle analysis; unlocking low carbon potential and carbon Vision Leadership Awards.

--- Figure **36**

Comparison of R&D Budgets as Percentage of GDP

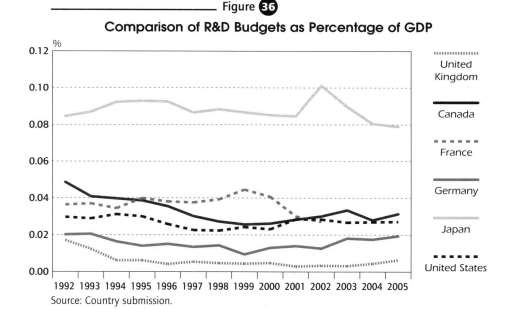

Source: Country submission.

INTERNATIONAL R&D COLLABORATION

The UK is very engaged in international collaboration on technology research and development including bilateral agreements and MoUs (*e.g.* UK/China collaboration, EU/China Near Zero Emissions Coal Project), active participation in multilateral programmes (*e.g.* ITER; Gen IV; IPHE; CSLF; and M2M) and international collaboration through the European Framework Programme.

The UK is participating in a number of IEA Implementing Agreements.

CRITIQUE

The government's position has been that energy technology research and development is primarily a matter for the energy industries themselves. Closure of research laboratories and privatisation have reduced government's engagement in technology development, and resulted in a significant decline in government's research expenditures throughout the 1980s and 1990s. The government supports principles of non-intervention and the use of market-based mechanisms to sustain deployment of new technologies to the market. The government is to be commended for its achievements as an international front runner in this respect.

However, the market-based policies have not ensured innovation and deployment of new energy technologies to address the long-term challenges facing the UK. Within existing frameworks, market actors have tended to pick mature cost-effective energy technologies like CCGT, landfill gas and wind. It is likely that both direct incentives for carbon reduction *and* incentives for innovation in lower carbon technology will be necessary. Government leadership will be needed to accelerate innovation and make new energy technologies available for the market. This leadership includes a coherent energy technology strategy with support for research, development, demonstration and deployment in line with energy policy objectives.

There are signs that the government is indeed taking on the responsibility of pursuing an active technology policy again. The Energy White Paper 2003 endorsed that increased RD&D effort was crucial to identifying new energy options and that energy research and its proper co-ordination should be key priorities for government. The UK's spending on RD&D is being raised. Establishment of the Carbon Trust, the UK Energy Research Centre, the Energy Research Partnerships, and the launch of a new National Institute of Energy Technology are all indications that the UK government is rebuilding its capacity for an active energy technology policy.

Rebuilding this capacity and engaging more in technology RD&D involves several challenges. Consistency and coherence are paramount to winning business confidence and bringing private funding to the table. Continued involvement of energy sector business in designing and implementing a coherent, cost-effective technology strategy is therefore considered to be crucial.

It has been difficult to get an overview of public RD&D spending in the UK or the consistency and coherence of the programmes. The research landscape seems crowded, fragmented and unco-ordinated, with the risk of gaps and/or overlaps. Lack of an overview of actors, funding mechanisms and good data on public research programmes makes it difficult for the government to evaluate and design effective RD&D programmes. The lack of overview is probably linked to the fact that no one organisation has overall responsibility for energy research, as is the case in many other IEA countries. Energy R&D is funded and prioritised through various actors, including DTI, Defra, DfT, ODPM, Regional Development Agencies, Carbon Trust and Research Councils. Priorities appear to be set by individual organisations within the context of their activities and needs.

The government is to be commended on its active support to international collaboration on R&D. UK international collaboration includes participation in Implementing Agreements within the IEA technology collaboration framework, in multilateral collaboration, like IPHE, CSLF, ITER, Generation IV International Forum, M2M, in the EU's Framework Programmes and ERA networks. The UK has several bilateral Memorandums of Understanding on research collaboration, *e.g.* with US, India and China.

RECOMMENDATIONS

The government of the United Kingdom should:

▶ *Clearly define the government's role in the development and innovation of energy technologies with a view towards promoting a more active role in support of research, development, demonstration and deployment of energy technologies.*

▶ *Develop a strategy for energy RD&D consistent with energy policy goals.*

▶ *Consider an increase in the government budget for research and development to align it more closely with that of other IEA member countries.*

▶ *Improve the oversight of public and privately funded RD&D (actors, funds, technologies) to enable the design of more cost-effective RD&D programmes and avoid overlap.*

▶ *Improve co-ordination between funding and priority-setting entities of public-funded energy RD&D programmes.*

▶ *Promote the role of the private sector in the definition and implementation of RD&D and continue to involve business in the design and targeting of public technology policy.*

▶ *Remain active in international collaboration to share technology development costs with other countries and to deal with problems that are essentially global, requiring significant funding over a long period of time.*

ENERGY BALANCES AND KEY STATISTICAL DATA

Unit: Mtoe

SUPPLY								
		1973	1990	2003	2004	2010	2020	2030
TOTAL PRODUCTION		**108.5**	**208.0**	**246.4**	**225.2**	..	..	..
Coal		75.9	53.6	16.8	14.9	..	..	..
Oil		0.5	95.2	110.7	99.6	..	..	..
Gas		24.4	40.9	92.6	86.4	..	..	..
Comb. Renewables & Waste[1]		–	0.6	2.8	2.9	8.9	12.9	..
Nuclear		7.3	17.1	23.1	20.8	18.2	7.7	..
Hydro		0.3	0.4	0.3	0.4	0.5	0.7	..
Geothermal		–	0.0	0.0	0.0	–	–	..
Solar/Wind/Other		–	0.0	0.1	0.2	1.0	1.5	..
TOTAL NET IMPORTS[2]		**110.4**	**2.1**	**-16.4**	**9.6**	..	..	..
Coal	Exports	2.0	1.8	0.5	0.6	..	..	..
	Imports	1.1	10.3	20.5	23.2	..	..	..
	Net Imports	–0.9	8.5	20.0	22.6	..	..	..
Oil	Exports	20.9	76.5	101.6	97.9	..	..	..
	Imports	136.9	65.4	73.9	84.7	..	..	..
	Bunkers	5.4	2.5	1.8	2.1	..	..	..
	Net Imports	110.6	–13.6	–29.5	–15.3	..	..	..
Gas	Exports	–	–	13.7	8.8	..	..	..
	Imports	0.7	6.2	6.7	10.3	..	..	..
	Net Imports	0.7	6.2	–7.0	1.5	..	..	..
Electricity	Exports	0.0	0.0	0.3	0.2	–	–	..
	Imports	0.0	1.0	0.4	0.8	0.7	0.7	..
	Net Imports	0.0	1.0	0.2	0.6	0.7	0.7	..
TOTAL STOCK CHANGES		**1.8**	**2.1**	**2.2**	**-1.1**	..	..	..
TOTAL SUPPLY (TPES)		**220.7**	**212.2**	**232.3**	**233.7**	**238.6**	**246.4**	..
Coal		76.4	63.1	38.1	37.5	37.6	29.9	..
Oil		111.6	82.6	81.8	83.7	86.9	95.9	..
Gas		25.1	47.2	85.9	87.4	84.8	97.1	..
Comb. Renewables & Waste[1]		–	0.6	2.8	3.1	8.9	12.9	..
Nuclear		7.3	17.1	23.1	20.8	18.2	7.7	..
Hydro		0.3	0.4	0.3	0.4	0.5	0.7	..
Geothermal		–	0.0	0.0	0.0	–	–	..
Solar/Wind/Other		–	0.0	0.1	0.2	1.0	1.5	..
Electricity Trade[3]		0.0	1.0	0.2	0.6	0.7	0.7	..
Shares (%)								
Coal		*34.6*	*29.7*	*16.4*	*16.0*	*15.8*	*12.1*	..
Oil		*50.5*	*38.9*	*35.2*	*35.8*	*36.4*	*38.9*	..
Gas		*11.4*	*22.2*	*37.0*	*37.4*	*35.5*	*39.4*	..
Comb. Renewables & Waste		–	*0.3*	*1.2*	*1.3*	*3.7*	*5.2*	..
Nuclear		*3.3*	*8.1*	*10.0*	*8.9*	*7.6*	*3.1*	..
Hydro		*0.2*	*0.2*	*0.1*	*0.2*	*0.2*	*0.3*	..
Geothermal		–	–	–	–	–	–	..
Solar/Wind/Other		–	–	*0.1*	*0.1*	*0.4*	*0.6*	..
Electricity Trade		–	*0.5*	*0.1*	*0.3*	*0.3*	*0.3*	..

0 is negligible, – is nil, .. is not available.

Please note: In the course of preparing UK energy projections, some off model adjustments to take account of prospective measures in the UK's Climate Change Programme have not necessarily been fully included in the CO_2 emissions projections. All forecasts are based on the 2004 submission.

DEMAND

FINAL CONSUMPTION BY SECTOR

	1973	1990	2003	2004	2010	2020	2030
TFC	**147.1**	**145.4**	**161.1**	**163.7**	**169.5**	**185.2**	..
Coal	26.5	10.8	2.6	3.0	6.3	6.3	..
Oil	77.0	68.8	75.1	77.3	80.6	89.8	..
Gas	23.6	41.8	51.8	51.2	52.4	56.3	..
Comb. Renewables & Waste[1]	–	0.4	0.7	0.7	–	–	..
Geothermal	–	0.0	0.0	0.0	–	–	..
Solar/Wind/Other	–	0.0	0.0	0.0	–	–	..
Electricity	20.0	23.6	29.0	29.2	30.2	32.8	..
Heat	–	–	1.9	2.2	..	..	..
Shares (%)							
Coal	*18.0*	*7.4*	*1.6*	*1.9*	*3.7*	*3.4*	..
Oil	*52.3*	*47.3*	*46.6*	*47.2*	*47.6*	*48.5*	..
Gas	*16.1*	*28.7*	*32.1*	*31.3*	*30.9*	*30.4*	..
Comb. Renewables & Waste	–	*0.3*	*0.4*	*0.4*	–	–	..
Geothermal	–	–	–	–	–	–	..
Solar/Wind/Other	–	–	–	–	–	–	..
Electricity	*13.6*	*16.2*	*18.0*	*17.9*	*17.8*	*17.7*	..
Heat	–	–	*1.2*	*1.3*	..	..	..
TOTAL INDUSTRY[4]	**65.0**	**42.8**	**44.2**	**44.2**	**48.8**	**52.2**	..
Coal	13.3	6.4	1.6	2.0	6.1	6.0	..
Oil	33.7	15.7	17.7	18.7	17.1	16.9	..
Gas	10.1	12.0	13.6	12.0	15.4	17.6	..
Comb. Renewables & Waste[1]	–	0.1	0.3	0.3	–	–	..
Geothermal	–	–	–	–	–	–	..
Solar/Wind/Other	–	–	–	–	–	–	..
Electricity	7.8	8.7	9.8	10.1	10.2	11.7	..
Heat	–	–	1.1	1.2	..	..	..
Shares (%)							
Coal	*20.5*	*14.9*	*3.6*	*4.4*	*12.5*	*11.5*	..
Oil	*51.8*	*36.8*	*40.0*	*42.2*	*35.0*	*32.4*	..
Gas	*15.6*	*27.9*	*30.9*	*27.2*	*31.6*	*33.7*	..
Comb. Renewables & Waste	–	*0.2*	*0.6*	*0.6*	–	–	..
Geothermal	–	–	–	–	–	–	..
Solar/Wind/Other	–	–	–	–	–	–	..
Electricity	*12.1*	*20.2*	*22.3*	*22.8*	*20.9*	*22.4*	..
Heat	–	–	*2.6*	*2.8*	..	..	..
TRANSPORT[5]	**31.0**	**46.5**	**53.5**	**54.8**	**59.4**	**68.2**	..
TOTAL OTHER SECTORS[6]	**51.2**	**56.1**	**63.4**	**64.6**	**61.3**	**64.8**	..
Coal	13.1	4.4	1.0	1.1	0.2	0.3	..
Oil	12.6	7.0	4.6	4.5	4.9	5.5	..
Gas	13.5	29.8	38.1	39.2	37.0	38.7	..
Comb. Renewables & Waste[1]	–	0.3	0.4	0.4	–	–	..
Geothermal	–	0.0	0.0	0.0	–	–	..
Solar/Wind/Other	–	0.0	0.0	0.0	–	–	..
Electricity	12.0	14.5	18.5	18.5	19.2	20.3	..
Heat	–	–	0.8	1.0	..	..	..
Shares (%)							
Coal	*25.5*	*7.8*	*1.6*	*1.7*	*0.3*	*0.5*	..
Oil	*24.7*	*12.5*	*7.3*	*6.9*	*8.0*	*8.5*	..
Gas	*26.4*	*53.2*	*60.1*	*60.7*	*60.4*	*59.7*	..
Comb. Renewables & Waste	–	*0.6*	*0.7*	*0.6*	–	–	..
Geothermal	–	–	–	–	–	–	..
Solar/Wind/Other	–	–	–	–	–	–	..
Electricity	*23.4*	*25.8*	*29.1*	*28.6*	*31.3*	*31.3*	..
Heat	–	–	*1.2*	*1.5*	..	..	..

DEMAND

ENERGY TRANSFORMATION AND LOSSES

	1973	1990	2003	2004	2010	2020	2030
ELECTRICITY GENERATION[7]							
INPUT (Mtoe)	72.5	74.4	85.3	84.3	81.6	79.2	..
OUTPUT (Mtoe)	24.2	27.3	34.1	33.8	34.4	37.1	..
(TWh gross)	281.4	317.8	395.9	393.2	400.4	432.0	..
Output Shares (%)							
Coal	*62.1*	*65.0*	*35.4*	*34.1*	*25.7*	*17.0*	..
Oil	*25.6*	*10.9*	*1.2*	*1.2*	*2.3*	*2.1*	..
Gas	*1.0*	*1.6*	*38.2*	*40.6*	*44.4*	*60.6*	..
Comb. Renewables & Waste	*–*	*0.2*	*1.7*	*2.0*	*5.7*	*7.5*	..
Nuclear	*10.0*	*20.7*	*22.4*	*20.3*	*17.5*	*6.8*	..
Hydro	*1.4*	*1.6*	*0.8*	*1.3*	*1.4*	*1.9*	..
Geothermal	*–*	*–*	*–*	*–*	*–*	*–*	..
Solar/Wind/Other	*–*	*0.0*	*0.3*	*0.5*	*3.0*	*4.1*	..
TOTAL LOSSES	75.2	67.5	71.0	70.0	69.1	61.2	..
of which:							
Electricity and Heat Generation[8]	48.3	47.1	49.4	48.3	47.2	42.0	..
Other Transformation	9.7	4.1	2.6	2.5	6.8	6.7	..
Own Use and Losses[9]	17.3	16.3	19.1	19.1	15.1	12.5	..
Statistical Differences	–1.7	–0.7	0.2	0.0	–	–	..

INDICATORS

	1973	1990	2003	2004P	2010	2020	2030
GDP (billion 2000 USD)	813.40	1130.90	1542.20	1591.10	1899.86	2431.98	..
Population (millions)	56.22	57.24	59.55	59.84	61.40	63.80	..
TPES/GDP[10]	0.27	0.19	0.15	0.15	0.13	0.10	..
Energy Production/TPES	0.49	0.98	1.06	0.96	..	..	..
Per Capita TPES[11]	3.93	3.71	3.90	3.91	3.89	3.86	..
Oil Supply/GDP[10]	0.14	0.07	0.05	0.05	0.05	0.04	..
TFC/GDP[10]	0.18	0.13	0.10	0.10	0.09	0.08	..
Per Capita TFC[11]	2.62	2.54	2.71	2.74	2.76	2.90	..
Energy-related CO_2 Emissions (Mt CO_2)[12]	640.1	557.6	534.3	537.1	541.3	561.4	..
CO2 Emissions from Bunkers (Mt CO_2)	25.4	23.6	35.3	39.4	39.3	50.3	..

GROWTH RATES (% per year)

	73–79	79–90	90–03	03–04	04–10	10–20	20–30
TPES	–0.1	–0.3	0.7	0.6	0.3	0.3	..
Coal	–0.5	–1.5	–3.8	–1.6	0.1	–2.3	..
Oil	–2.6	–1.3	–0.1	2.2	0.6	1.0	..
Gas	8.3	1.4	4.7	1.8	–0.5	1.4	..
Comb. Renewables & Waste	–	–	12.1	10.8	19.4	3.8	..
Nuclear	5.4	5.0	2.3	–9.8	–2.2	–8.3	..
Hydro	1.6	1.9	–3.6	52.5	2.0	3.8	..
Geothermal	–	–	–	–	–	–	..
Solar/Wind/Other	–	–	21.0	45.8	32.7	3.8	..
TFC	0.1	–0.2	0.8	1.6	0.6	0.9	..
Electricity Consumption	0.9	1.0	1.6	0.8	0.5	0.8	..
Energy Production	10.1	0.7	1.3	–8.6	–	–	..
Net Oil Imports	–27.1	–	6.1	–48.0	–	–	..
GDP	1.5	2.2	2.4	3.2	3.0	2.5	..
Growth in the TPES/GDP Ratio	–1.6	–2.5	–1.7	–2.5	–2.6	–2.1	..
Growth in the TFC/GDP Ratio	–1.4	–2.3	–1.6	–1.5	–2.3	–1.6	..

Please note: Rounding may cause totals to differ from the sum of the elements.

FOOTNOTES TO ENERGY BALANCES
AND KEY STATISTICAL DATA

1   Comprises solid biomass, biogas, industrial waste and municipal waste. Data are often based on partial surveys and may not be comparable between countries.

2   Total net imports include combustible renewables and waste.

3   Total supply of electricity represents net trade. A negative number indicates that exports are greater than imports.

4   Includes non-energy use.

5   Includes less than 1% non-oil fuels.

6   Includes residential, commercial, public service and agricultural sectors.

7   Inputs to electricity generation include inputs to electricity, CHP and heat plants. Output refers only to electricity generation.

8   Losses arising in the production of electricity and heat at main activity producer utilities (formerly known as public) and autoproducers. For non-fossil-fuel electricity generation, theoretical losses are shown based on plant efficiencies of 33% for nuclear and 100% for hydro.

9   Data on "losses" for forecast years often include large statistical differences covering differences between expected supply and demand and mostly do not reflect real expectations on transformation gains and losses.

10 Toe per thousand US dollars at 2000 prices and exchange rates.

11 Toe per person.

12 "Energy-related CO_2 emissions" have been estimated using the IPCC Tier I Sectoral Approach. In accordance with the IPCC methodology, emissions from international marine and aviation bunkers are not included in national totals. Projected emissions for oil and gas are derived by calculating the ratio of emissions to energy use for 2004 and applying this factor to forecast energy supply. Future coal emissions are based on product-specific supply projections and are calculated using the IPCC/OECD emission factors and methodology.

INTERNATIONAL ENERGY AGENCY "SHARED GOALS"

The 26 member countries* of the International Energy Agency (IEA) seek to create the conditions in which the energy sectors of their economies can make the fullest possible contribution to sustainable economic development and the well-being of their people and of the environment. In formulating energy policies, the establishment of free and open markets is a fundamental point of departure, though energy security and environmental protection need to be given particular emphasis by governments. IEA countries recognise the significance of increasing global interdependence in energy. They therefore seek to promote the effective operation of international energy markets and encourage dialogue with all participants.

In order to secure their objectives they therefore aim to create a policy framework consistent with the following goals:

1. **Diversity, efficiency and flexibility within the energy sector** are basic conditions for longer-term energy security: the fuels used within and across sectors and the sources of those fuels should be as diverse as practicable. Non-fossil fuels, particularly nuclear and hydro power, make a substantial contribution to the energy supply diversity of IEA countries as a group.

2. Energy systems should have **the ability to respond promptly and flexibly to energy emergencies.** In some cases this requires collective mechanisms and action: IEA countries co-operate through the Agency in responding jointly to oil supply emergencies.

3. **The environmentally sustainable provision and use of energy** is central to the achievement of these shared goals. Decision-makers should seek to minimise the adverse environmental impacts of energy activities, just as environmental decisions should take account of the energy consequences. Government interventions should where practicable have regard to the Polluter Pays Principle.

4. **More environmentally acceptable energy sources** need to be encouraged and developed. Clean and efficient use of fossil fuels is essential. The development of economic non-fossil sources is also a priority. A number of IEA members wish to retain and improve the nuclear

---

* Australia, Austria, Belgium, Canada, the Czech Republic, Denmark, Finland, France, Germany, Greece, Hungary, Ireland, Italy, Japan, Korea, Luxembourg, the Netherlands, New Zealand, Norway, Portugal, Spain, Sweden, Switzerland, Turkey, the United Kingdom, the United States.

option for the future, at the highest available safety standards, because nuclear energy does not emit carbon dioxide. Renewable sources will also have an increasingly important contribution to make.

5. **Improved energy efficiency** can promote both environmental protection and energy security in a cost-effective manner. There are significant opportunities for greater energy efficiency at all stages of the energy cycle from production to consumption. Strong efforts by governments and all energy users are needed to realise these opportunities.

6. Continued **research, development and market deployment of new and improved energy technologies** make a critical contribution to achieving the objectives outlined above. Energy technology policies should complement broader energy policies. International co-operation in the development and dissemination of energy technologies, including industry participation and co-operation with non-member countries, should be encouraged.

7. **Undistorted energy prices** enable markets to work efficiently. Energy prices should not be held artificially below the costs of supply to promote social or industrial goals. To the extent necessary and practicable, the environmental costs of energy production and use should be reflected in prices.

8. **Free and open trade** and a secure framework for investment contribute to efficient energy markets and energy security. Distortions to energy trade and investment should be avoided.

9. **Co-operation among all energy market participants** helps to improve information and understanding, and encourage the development of efficient, environmentally acceptable and flexible energy systems and markets worldwide. These are needed to help promote the investment, trade and confidence necessary to achieve global energy security and environmental objectives.

(The Shared Goals were adopted by IEA Ministers at their 4 June 1993 meeting in Paris.)

GLOSSARY AND LIST OF ABBREVIATIONS

In this report, abbreviations are substituted for a number of terms used within the International Energy Agency. While these terms generally have been written out on first mention in each chapter, this glossary provides a quick and central reference for many of the abbreviations used.

ACS	average cold spell
AGR	Advanced Gas Reactors
BETTA	British Electricity Trading and Transmission Arrangements
BP	British Petroleum
bcm	billion cubic metres
b/d	barrels per day
cal	calorie
CCA	Climate Change Agreements
CCGT	combined-cycle gas turbine
CCL	Climate Change Levy
CCS	carbon capture and storage
CCP	Climate Change Programme
CEGB	Central Electric Generating Board
CERT	Committee on Energy Research and Technology of the IEA
CFCs	chlorofluorocarbons
CHP	combined production of heat and power; sometimes, when referring to industrial CHP, the term "co-generation" is used
CNG	compressed natural gas
CO	carbon monoxide
CO_2	carbon dioxide
cm	cubic metre
DC	direct current
DH	district heating
DSO	distribution system operator

ECA	enhanced capital allowances
EEC	Energy Efficiency Commitment
EFTA	European Free Trade Association: Iceland, Norway, Switzerland and Liechtenstein
EIA	environmental impact assessment
EST	Energy Saving Trust
ETSO	European Transmission System Operators Group
EU	The European Union, whose members are Austria, Belgium, Bulgaria, Cyprus, the Czech Republic, Denmark, Estonia, Finland, France, Germany, Greece, Hungary, Ireland, Italy, Latvia, Lithuania, Luxembourg, Malta, the Netherlands, Poland, Portugal, Romania, the Slovak Republic, Slovenia, Spain, Sweden and the United Kingdom
EUP	energy-using products
Euro	European currency (€)
FCCC	Framework Convention on Climate Change
FGD	fuel gas desulphurisation
FSU	former Soviet Union
GDP	gross domestic product
GNP	gross national product
GEF	Global Environmental Facility
GJ	gigajoule, or 1 joule $\times 10^9$
GW	gigawatt, or 1 watt $\times 10^9$
GWh	gigawatt x one hour, or one watt x one hour $\times 10^9$
HGV	heavy goods vehicules
IAEA	International Atomic Energy Agency
IEA	International Energy Agency whose members are Australia, Austria, Belgium, Canada, the Czech Republic, Denmark, Finland, France, Germany, Greece, Hungary, Ireland, Italy, Japan, Korea, Luxembourg, the Netherlands, New Zealand, Norway, Portugal, Spain, Sweden, Switzerland, Turkey, the United Kingdom, the United States
IEP	International Energy Program, one of the founding documents of the IEA
IGCC	integrated coal gasification combined cycle plant
IPCC	International Panel on Climate Change
ISO	independent system operator

J	joule; a joule is the work done when the point of application of a force of one newton is displaced through a distance of one metre in the direction of the force (a newton is defined as the force needed to accelerate a kilogram by one metre per second). In electrical units, it is the energy dissipated by one watt in a second
kV	kilovolt, or one volt $\times 10^3$
kWh	kilowatt-hour, or one kilowatt $\times$ one hour, or one watt $\times$ one hour $\times 10^3$
LDC	local distribution company
LNG	liquefied natural gas
LPG	liquefied petroleum gas; refers to propane, butane and their isomers, which are gases at atmospheric pressure and normal temperature
mcm	million cubic metres
MID	Market Index Data.
Mt	million tonnes
$MtCO_2$	million tonnes of CO_2
Mtoe	million tonnes of oil equivalent; see toe
MTP	Market Transformation Programme
MW	megawatt of electricity, or 1 Watt $\times 10^6$
MWh	megawatt-hour = one megawatt $\times$ one hour, or one watt $\times$ one hour $\times 10^6$
NAP	National Allocation Plan
NDA	Nuclear Decommissioning Authority
NEA	Nuclear Energy Agency of the OECD
negTPA	negotiated third-party access
NETA	New Electricity Trading Arrangements
NO_x	nitrogen oxides
OECD	Organisation for Economic Co-operation and Development
OTC	over the counter
p	pence
PJ	petajoule, or 1 joule $\times 10^{15}$
ppm	parts per million
PPP	purchasing power parity: the rate of currency conversion that equalises the purchasing power of different currencies, *i.e.* estimates the differences in price levels between different countries

PRT	Petroleum Revenue Tax
PWR	Pressurised Water Reactor
regTPA	regulated third-party access
R&D	research and development, especially in energy technology; may include the demonstration and dissemination phases as well
RO	Renewables Obligation
ROC	Renewables Oblication Certificate
TRFO	Renewable Transport Fuel Obligation
SB	single buyer
SDC	Sustainable Development Commission
SLT	Standing Group on Long-Term Co-operation of the IEA
SMEs	small and medium-sized enterprises
SO_2	sulphur dioxide
SYS	Seven Year Statement
TFC	total final consumption of energy; the difference between TPES and TFC consists of net energy losses in the production of electricity and synthetic gas, refinery use and other energy sector uses and losses
TNUoS	Transmission Network Use of System
toe	tonne of oil equivalent, defined as 10^7 kcal
TOP	take-or-pay contract
TPA	third-party access
TPES	total primary energy supply
TSO	transmission system operator
TW	terawatt, or 1 watt $\times$ 10^{12}
TWh	terawatt $\times$ one hour, or one watt x one hour $\times$ 10^{12}
UGS	underground storage (of natural gas)
UKCS	United Kingdom Continental Shelf
UN	the United Nations Organisation
VAT	value-added tax
VED	vehicule excise duty
VOCs	volatile organic compounds

The Online Bookshop

IEA PUBLICATIONS, 9, rue de la Fédération, 75739 PARIS CEDEX 15
PRINTED IN FRANCE BY STEDI MEDIA
(61 2006 07 1P1) ISBN : 92-64-1097-73 – 2007